CW00661953

DAVID NORRIS

Growthadox

Embracing Paradox to Unlock Personal and Business Growth. A how-to guide for startup founders, growth leaders and entrepreneurs.

Copyright © 2023 by David Norris

All rights reserved. No part of this publication may be reproduced, stored or transmitted in any form or by any means, electronic, mechanical, photocopying, recording, scanning, or otherwise without written permission from the publisher. It is illegal to copy this book, post it to a website, or distribute it by any other means without permission.

David Norris asserts the moral right to be identified as the author of this work.

David Norris has no responsibility for the persistence or accuracy of URLs for external or third-party Internet Websites referred to in this publication and does not guarantee that any content on such Websites is, or will remain, accurate or appropriate.

Designations used by companies to distinguish their products are often claimed as trademarks. All brand names and product names used in this book and on its cover are trade names, service marks, trademarks and registered trademarks of their respective owners. The publishers and the book are not associated with any product or vendor mentioned in this book. None of the companies referenced within the book have endorsed the book.

First edition

This book was professionally typeset on Reedsy.
Find out more at reedsy.com

"I started out with nothing, and I still got most of it left."

SEASICK STEVE

Contents

Preface

Growth (whether personal or business) often involves paradoxes, such as the need to let go of old beliefs and habits in order to embrace new ones, or the importance of facing challenges and setbacks in order to grow stronger and more resilient.

The Cambridge Dictionary defines the verb "to grow" as:

> "To increase in size or amount, or to become more advanced or developed."

Growth is a word we use in everyday conversation assuming that the meaning is well understood. Yes, the dictionary definition is a good start but I tend to think about growth in a different way.

In physics there is a concept of entropy. I'm no physicist but the way I understand it is that entropy relates to the amount of disorder in a system. The universe is in a gradual state of increasing entropy; it is trending towards decay and disorder. In other words, all other things being equal, things will decay. To keep anything going in a steady state requires energy and attention. A human being needs feeding and a golf green needs mowing. A car needs servicing and a dog needs exercise. Without these, decay happens. Growth however, is more than standing still. It's moving forwards and ahead. It's keeping the steady state going and going further. If it takes energy to stand still, it takes even more to move ahead.

A business succeeds if (at a minimum) it has a product or service to sell to customers that meets their needs. Given that technology, the market, customer needs and trading conditions change on a daily basis, a business needs to continually adapt to maintain its performance. That requires energy and investment. As any swimmer will know, treading water still takes energy and effort. To swim requires additional effort, and so does growth.

I see this to be the case on a personal level too. Staying relevant and being skilled for the work needed requires continual effort. Without effort we will decay. I know that if I had the skills I had 30 years ago I would not be able to succeed in today's world doing the job I had 30 years ago. To move ahead means staying up to date and developing new skills and experience above and beyond keeping up.

Growth therefore is winning against entropy. If you agree with me, then you'll also understand that it is only a temporary gain. No company survives forever and neither will you or I. However, paradoxically it's the only meaningful approach to life. Choose decay, choose treading water or choose growth. With a growth mindset you can make a difference and have an impact. However it's the hard path, not the easy life.

Why does a child build a sand castle on the beach? Moreover, why do adults? I love creating a sand castle if I go to a sandy beach. I know very well that the tide will destroy my creation but creativity is its own reward. Such is life. We build our metaphorical sand castles knowing that the tide will sweep everything away.

Throughout my 30-plus year career, I've discovered that the journey towards growth is never-ending. The more I've learned and achieved, the more I've realised how much there is still left to accomplish. This is the first paradox of growth: the more we know, the more we realise we don't know.

Growth inevitably involves discomfort. It involves taking risks and facing into the wind, choosing the more difficult path. Growth is never easy. It's always hard-won.

Sporting champions are often the athletes who are prepared to train harder and suffer more than any of their competitors. Successful startups are few and far between. More than two-thirds never deliver a positive return to their investors. The ones that do work incredibly hard (and smart) to win. Founders are passionate about their cause and will suffer to succeed. In fact, the word passion is derived from the Latin word "passio", which means to suffer and endure.

(At the extreme, growth in one domain or area might be at the expense of others. For example, career success can take its toll on family life if not managed carefully.)

Some of the biggest growth opportunities that I've had on a personal level also involved some kind of suffering, such as taking on emotional risk, working through a crisis or facing a problem rather than shying away from it. Sometimes it's those situations that you most fear that give you the biggest opportunity for growth. Growth is never handed to you on a plate.

This book explores growth and some of its associated paradoxes and contradictions. I'll share my insights on how to embrace paradoxes to continue growing as a business leader. I hope these tips - from strategic thinking to team leadership and personal effectiveness - can help you unlock your full potential and achieve sustained business and personal growth.

This book is not a book (paradox number one). This book is in fact a series of articles that are based on blogs I've written over the past 15 years. Every so often I would have an idea or a thought and I sought to capture it like a butterfly in a net before it flew away. By writing it down, I could then study it. It turns out that writing things down is good for thinking. And thinking is good for writing things down.

Some of these ideas were triggered by things I read, some by conversations with colleagues or friends. I can't say any of these ideas are uniquely mine. All I did was write them down.

Recently, with the benefit of hindsight and distance, I've realised that there was a common thread binding much (but not all) of my writing. Like the Taoist philosophical concept of Yin and Yang, I've found that there are often two sides to every coin. The language of our western culture has often dealt in opposites (night and day, good and bad, fast and slow etc.) whereas I hope to see reality in a more nuanced way than simple black and white or right and wrong. I've always felt that the world is more like shades of the rainbow. Night and day can't exist without each other, neither can energy and rest or work and play. The borders between each are fuzzy and often one is just the inverse of the other.

To move forward in one area might mean accepting a trade off in another area. There are always two sides to a coin. You might find you can unlock growth by considering both sides. Sometimes, approaching a problem from a counterintuitive direction can yield rich insight and opportunity.

Caroline Clark, a good friend, ex-colleague (and now product coach), illustrated this point for me with this Buddhist concept:

> "When does a seed become a plant? We know it does because it grows. And if you sliced it down into separate timestamps you would see first it's a seed in the ground, then a seed germinating, then a sprout, then a small plant, then a larger plant etc. There is no single transition where it goes from being a seed in one moment to a plant in the next, but a series of transitions that we arbitrarily break down through time measurement. It is a plant because it is not a seed, and vice versa."

In life - and in business - understanding these nuances of paradox can make the difference between success and failure, growth and stagnation. It means that often we have to do something counterintuitive to move forward.

I seek to surface some of these seeming contradictions. The paradoxes that I've experienced and about which I write have helped me find my way in life and in my career. I've found myself working in fast-moving growth companies in the internet age. I didn't have a plan to do that. My only plan was to work hard on things I was interested in; somehow, over the years, I moved forward and learned a few lessons on the way.

Note, however, that my insights and observations are based purely on my experience to date, so should not be taken as exhaustive or complete. There are probably many more paradoxes out there that I have not yet encountered.

I've grouped the articles into four sections:

- Finding growth
- Unlocking growth
- Delivering growth
- Personal growth

You should be able to dip into any section in any order. You don't need to read cover to cover. Each article should make sense on its own. If you do read all the articles in a section, I hope that the whole is greater than the sum of the parts and that you find a big picture that makes sense for you.

"Vision without execution is hallucination."

I love this quote. I believe it was Thomas Edison who first popularised it. My career as a business builder has led me to focus not only on where to find opportunities for growth but how to deliver it. In my experience, the boundaries between the two are sometimes blurred. You'll find therefore that much of this book is about how to operationalise growth - how to organise your team to execute on a plan and how to make the most of the talent you have available. Having great ideas is never enough - it's putting them into practice that counts. And I think about growth in the widest sense of the word: growth for your venture, your team and yourself.

I also can only write about what I know. For example, I have very little experience of B2B businesses, large corporations, regulated businesses, public companies and government institutions. I have mainly worked in fast-growth consumer internet businesses so there's a bias towards examples from that sphere.

There's not necessarily a paradox in every article. What I hope to illustrate through the book is that you can build a growth mindset by appreciating that sometimes the best path forward may be a counterintuitive one. A growth mindset requires looking at the world in a nuanced way and working through problems in non-obvious ways. It's a curious, maverick mindset that struggles with settling for the status quo and is prepared to take risks. You need to look at both sides of every coin.

By pulling my thoughts together in this short volume, I hope I can help you on your own journey - of making something of life, of doing well for yourself, your family and your community, and of making your own mark on the world.

Maybe this is volume one. Maybe at a later date there will be a volume two. Maybe not.

Thanks for reading. I hope you find it useful.

David Norris
    Deal, Kent, 2023.

1

Introduction

I started on this book after I'd finished writing most of it. Long before I decided to create it, I'd already written down most of the thoughts contained here.

So we are starting at the end. We're always at the end of everything we've ever done. Yet everything we have yet to do hasn't happened yet. At least not in this version of your reality. Which is amazing. So much can yet come to be - and there is a lot you can do about it.

Knowing nothing is good for something

I consider myself both fortunate and lucky. I am grateful that I went to a decent school and had a good education. Yet as I look now at how I see the world versus how it was explained to me, there's a big difference.

In a secondary comprehensive school in Sheffield in the 1980s, I was ignorant of how the world really works.

They didn't teach me how businesses actually work - what marketing and operations are, how financial reports work, or the difference between revenue and cash, etc. It took many years for me to find this out.

They didn't teach me that you don't have to make a career choice, but that your career can choose you. You just need to try different things and find out what you're good at. I've had a very squiggly career path - see the next article, *To be certain of opportunity, choose uncertainty.*

They didn't teach me that there is no right answer. There can be many ways to solve a problem and it's your job to figure it out.

They didn't teach me that small companies are very different from big ones. I find I thrive in small to medium-sized companies. I look for roles with some degree of autonomy and personal challenge, and which allow me to play to my strengths.

They didn't teach me that success in a career is mostly the result of pure hard work while being trustworthy and approachable, but that you still need luck. It turns out you can put yourself in situations that increase your chance of receiving good luck.

They didn't teach me that you define what success is for you. No-one else.

They didn't teach me that you are the only person who can make yourself happy. No-one else.

They didn't teach me that on any journey you need to overcome obstacles. Developing the ability and willingness to navigate obstacles is an absolute must to grow a business and to grow as a person. Tenacity gets you a long way.

They didn't teach me that your biggest advantage is not your experience or knowledge, it's your curiosity. "Why can't we do it this way?" is more powerful than "It should be done this way."

They didn't teach me that best practice is like looking in the rear-view mirror.

There is always a better way. Best practice is only the best *so far*.

There's so much they didn't teach me that I marvel I managed to do anything in my career at all. It turns out that knowing nothing is good for something. Knowing nothing causes you to ask questions, be curious and have a go. Knowing nothing reduces fear of failure and fuels experimentation.

The paradox is that to grow and thrive, knowing too much can be a hindrance.

Sometimes it can be better to approach a problem from first principles and understand its root causes rather than assume you already know how to solve the problem. Instead of seeing your lack of knowledge or experience as a disadvantage, you can see it as an advantage, giving you a fresh perspective of embracing curiosity.

To be certain of opportunity, choose uncertainty

Were you ever asked, "What would you like to be when you grow up?" I was. I never had a good answer. I still don't know the answer.

I was however interested in getting out of Sheffield and I liked the idea of working for a travel company.

So, out of university, I worked on a French campsite cleaning tents and mobile homes for Eurocamp, a British tour operator. In the winter I washed dishes in a hotel in a French ski resort. I guess I started at the bottom, although I didn't see it that way. I was getting a chance to live and work overseas, and I was doing something I loved - providing great service to people on their holidays.

A ski anecdote: one night my good friend Robin (a.k.a. "Cactus") and I were planning our ski route for the following day. Robin said something that always stuck with me: "Remember, the only thing you can rely on [pause for effect]… is gravity." I don't know why, I just love that phrase. It's almost a personal mantra for me and if I were to have a tombstone, that's what I'd want engraved on it. It just reminds me that everything is transient and that everything we take for granted could easily be taken away.

The great thing about seasonal work is that it is an environment for opportunity. That's because most workers would only do one or two seasons, so if you came back, you were already one of the most experienced members of the team and therefore had a chance of taking on additional responsibility. Through hard work and just turning up each season, I was promoted. After four years, I ended up running operations as an area manager - in South West France for Eurocamp and all over the Alps for Simply Ski. At the age of 24, I was already managing 90 people. When I came back to the UK at the age of 26, I became an operations manager at Simply Ski, managing a team of 120 people across nine countries.

In 2000, I was very interested in getting involved with the internet as it was a new frontier with huge potential. I left my operations director role and took a pay cut to join a startup (ifyouski.com) as a product manager (although that job title didn't exist in 2000). I worked with a team of four developers to design and build a ski holiday booking system and the fulfillment relationship with a specialist travel agency.

Even though I went to university after school and acquired a degree - in Religious Studies - I have never used it. Instead, I have learned on the job throughout my career, turning my hand to whatever was needed at the time. I built my own website in HTML/ASP in 2002 to learn how it works (using a text editor, coding by hand). I learned email and pay-per-click (PPC) marketing at Online Travel Corporation; web analytics at lastminute.com; user research and SEO at Expedia; people/HR at Bookatable; fundraising and the recruitment of hundreds of people at a number of startups; contact centre operations at HouseTrip; and investing in startups at Forward Partners (where I was a venture capital partner). In 2008, I completed a Diploma in Company Direction from the Institute of Directors - much more useful than my degree.

Everyone who is an expert wasn't born one. Learn by doing, apply yourself and you'd be amazed at what you can learn. The best opportunities come when the company you are working for is going through change, so embrace uncertainty - it's your friend. Uncertainty provides opportunities for growth. I've always been drawn to new things. Maybe it's my impulsive, impetuous nature. Maybe it's an adventurous streak and a thirst for risk taking.

I'm still not an expert in anything - I'm a generalist and I still have loads to learn. But I do know how to apply myself to a problem, get stuck in, ask questions and have a go. The best place to do this is an environment of uncertainty.

What you fear most holds the greatest treasure

More than 150 years ago, British mountaineer Edward Whymper led a party of six climbers to the summit of the Matterhorn in Switzerland.

At 4,478m, the Matterhorn is not the highest mountain in the Alps, nor indeed in Switzerland, but its distinctive shape (famously found on Toblerone chocolate bars and Caran d'Ache pencil boxes, amongst others) makes it the most iconic.

It's a steep scramble up a knife-edge ridge that is often covered in snow and ice approaching the summit. I've never done it myself, but a good friend has.

Whymper's group made it to the top but only two of the party returned alive. After an hour of soaking up the summit, the team of six started their descent. Soon after, one of the party slipped, falling onto another and then dragging two more from the mountain. The rope snapped under the strain, leaving

Whymper to return to the valley with just one other member of his party. It was hardly a victory celebration, and the accident would haunt him for the rest of his life.

Controversy ensued. Was the rope cut? Nothing was ever proven. Why were so many young Englishmen risking their lives for this mountaineering folly?

Growth often comes at a cost. It requires effort and facing fear.
It's the very risk that can make the endeavour thrilling.
It's battling your internal demons to push on and succeed.
It's using the resources at your disposal to reach your goal.
It's standing on summits that are only gained through hard effort.
It's doing what most other people wouldn't dare dream of.

There are many parallels between mountaineering and entrepreneurship. Like mountaineers, entrepreneurs too have their own summits to reach. To do it alone is difficult. It's best to go as a team and it's good to be prepared.

Whymper wrote in his book, *Scrambles Amongst the Alps*...

> "Climb if you will, but remember that courage and strength are nought without prudence, and that a momentary negligence may destroy the happiness of a lifetime. Do nothing in haste; look well to each step; and from the beginning think what may be the end."

As you embrace growth, the paradox is that while you seek higher ground to stand on and the reward of doing so, getting there can be unpleasant and daunting.

Fear has a purpose. It is there to protect you and keep you safe. At some level you sense danger, whether that be physical, emotional or social, and your brain is acting on hundreds of thousands of years worth of evolutionary adaption to shield you from it. We easily imagine the worst. What you fear often provides an opportunity for growth.

For example, most people have a fear of public speaking. Even experienced speakers can fear going on stage. Good speakers only become good speakers through practice. Very few of us are natural-born orators. It's a learned skill and it requires practice. All great speakers had to start somewhere and they probably feared speaking as much as anyone else. However, they had the courage to face that fear and give it a go.

Going into this place where we face our fears is like entering a cave.

There's a scene in the movie *The Empire Strikes Back* when the young hero, Luke Skywalker, is being trained by the master Jedi, Yoda. There is a dark cave that Yoda urges Skywalker to enter and where he will battle evil.

Yoda says: "That place... is strong with the dark side of the Force. A domain of evil it is. In you must go."

"What's in there?" asks Luke

"Only what you take with you," replies Yoda

It's a way of saying that only by facing your fears you will find what you are looking for. Your strengths lie in overcoming your fears.

Next time you feel that fear, no matter how small, think about it as an opportunity. The fear is a signal that if you can be brave and face that fear, you can unlock an opportunity to grow.

Feel the fear and do it anyway.

Business growth leads to personal growth leads to business growth

Why am I writing about business growth and personal growth in the same book?

I've found that it is when we are tested that we build our experience and we learn. This testing could be creative, physical, emotional or intellectual. In a testing situation, you succeed or fail (or a combination of the two) and out of that situation you can improve your skills, knowledge and ability.

I've never really subscribed to the saying "What doesn't kill you makes you stronger." That seems too blunt, too simple. There are plenty of things that don't kill you but which can leave you weaker: abuse, war, terrible disease and so on. But then again, the saying hits home and it is memorable because we all recognise that tough situations can be an opportunity to learn and grow. It's also a reminder of the power of hope; no matter how difficult the situation, hope keeps us going and it can be an amazing motivator through the hard times.

Business growth is definitely not easy. It's like swimming against the tide. There are always things that go wrong, things that you don't expect. Sometimes a crisis can feel like too much to bear, stressful beyond belief. These challenges however teach you lessons and, as a result, you can grow as a person, as a team or as a business. I say can - not will - because how you adapt to these challenges will determine whether you respond to the stress and learn, or whether you stay set in your ways.

Business challenges can provide a crucible for personal growth. When I was working in a fast-growing scale-up, I certainly appreciated that. (A scale-up is a startup that is in a fast growth phase - more on that later.) Working one year in that environment is a multiplier. It can give you many times more experience than you'd get in a steady job at an established company in a similar amount of time. I always used to joke that startup years are like dog years. By the time you get to seven years, it feels like a lifetime.

Companies are, at the end of the day, a collection of people. People with emotions, daily struggles, ambition, hope, despair, energy and confusion. Good people trying to do good things most of the time. To improve the business, to find growth, means improving the people in the business. And if you are a leader of the business, how you are, how you approach your work, your team and your customers, will contribute to the success of that business and team.

So you can't grow a business to its full potential without the team of people in the business growth working to their own full potential. And if they do, they will create new business opportunities and these new business challenges will provide opportunities for them all to grow and learn.

Just as you can jump into the fire (metaphorically speaking) to create more opportunities for your own growth, you can fuel the fire through your own personal development.

That's why both topics are covered in this book. I just couldn't see a valid reason to disconnect the two. My writing over the years is a reflection of that reality and so this book looks at both.

2

Part 1: Finding growth - Understanding where to focus your energy

Which entrepreneur gave us the following advice?

> "The clear vision is important - then you keep pressing on, or indecision takes place. Of course you have to be prepared to change plans - it's a balance. Be inflexible and drive on into trouble, be a ditherer and get nowhere. You have to get the balance right."

Is this the founder of Tesla, Elon Musk, talking? Facebook's Mark Zuckerberg? Or was it Anita Roddick, the renowned founder of The Body Shop?

None of the above. It was in fact not an entrepreneur at all. It was British Everest mountaineer Chris Bonington.

Bonington was talking about the challenges in the mountains on reaching an objective, summit or route. Such expeditions are arduous and unpredictable, and require courage and good judgement as well as luck to succeed.

This is no different in business, or life in general for that matter. No matter what your objective, to get started you need to take the first steps. But also be aware that your challenge will likely change as you approach your goal. For example, if you decide to launch a new product, your efforts (in this case, to change what people buy in a specific product category) may trigger a response from competitors. Your strategy must change accordingly.

So make a plan, then make a plan B and be prepared to come up with plan C on the fly. Then put your best foot forward and get going.

Before we get into specifics, let's stay at a high level. What is growth and where does it come from?

I would suggest that at the very least there are three rules of thumb:

1. Solve real problems.
2. Reduce friction.
3. Aim to change your customer's behaviour.

Let's look at each of them.

Solve real problems

Real problems don't just come and go. They are there for the long term. They may be solved differently over the decades or centuries. By problem, I mean a situation which presents an opportunity. I'm using the word "problem" in a very wide sense. Therefore, the problem could be a customer simply having unmet needs, wants or desires.

For example, one problem I can think of has been solved four different ways since I was born. In the 1960s it was solved by the transistor radio. In the 1980s it was solved by the Sony Walkman. In the 2000s it was solved by the Apple iPod. And most recently it's been solved by Spotify.

The problem? A desire to listen to personalised music on the move. Each technological innovation (radio, cassette tapes, MP3, streaming) led to a new way in which the problem could be solved. That problem will continue to be solved in new ways as technology develops. Each new technological advancement is an opportunity for an entrepreneur to solve the problem in a new way that the customer values.

Here's another example that is more than 400 years old.

Mail coach. Telegram. Telephone. Whats App.

What's the problem? Demand for sending messages as quickly as possible.

Most of the advances in technology have simply mechanised or digitised a solution to an existing human need. Human needs are therefore predictable and you only need to look at existing solutions (analogue or digital) to see what people value. Often, it's a reduction in effort, but it could be joy, speed or insight. Anything that has value can create value. And growth comes from finding that value and extracting it.

A few other examples of how technology has changed solutions:

- A blog is just a digital diary.
- A news app is just a digital newspaper.
- An online travel agent is a digital travel shop.
- A telephone is a two-way audio telegraph.
- An iPhone is a digital telephone.
- A typewriter is a mechanical pen.
- A laptop is a digital typewriter.

Reduce friction

If you can make something easier, it has value. We are lazy, impatient, fickle creatures.

It's my view that almost every interesting innovation in business and in life is centred somehow around making things easier.

If you can make something easier, it has value.

Most advances in reducing friction come from technology creating new possibilities.

Humans have developed different technologies throughout the ages, and these have triggered revolutions and advances in progress each time.

First there was fire, then later came tools, agriculture, the wheel and simple machines. After that came steam power and then electricity-powered machines. Then came electronics, computing and the internet. Next will be artificial intelligence and artificial reality.

We are living through the digital revolution, and we are about to live through the AI revolution.

If we can use new software, solutions, services, machines, technology or methods, we can reduce friction. If we reduce friction on a problem that customers care about and are willing to pay to have solved, we can generate value and growth.

Change behaviour

Lastly, the third principle - change behaviour.

The very best companies change how their customers behave. Their innovations change their customers' lives.

Here are some examples.

Costa Coffee created a network of nationwide coffee vending machines, situated in high-transit locations such as service stations. It also introduced a loyalty app which rewards customers with a free drink for every 10 purchases. With this, Costa Coffee has changed the behaviour of its customers (including me), who now stop at Costa on their way to work to buy a coffee quickly and easily.

Uber changed the way customers use taxis. No longer do customers need to stand on a street corner to hail a cab or call to book one. They can simply (depending on their location) open the Uber app and request a ride on demand. Nor do they need to pay for their ride in cash or card on leaving the vehicle. It's all taken care of when their account is debited automatically. This leads to some customers choosing Uber as their first choice of travel, thereby changing their behaviours and habits.

Eurocamp is a company that rents camping pitches on high-quality campsites and then provides ready-equipped tents and mobile homes for customers to use. Families that would not otherwise consider camping due to the bother of buying, carrying and setting up their own camping equipment can now simply rent it and enjoy camping without the hassle.

In all these examples, the product or service has changed the way customers behave. This demonstrates value and is a useful acid test. "Will this change the behaviours of my customers in a positive way?" is a useful question to help you steer business growth.

Changing behaviour is easier said than done. We are creatures of habit and there needs to be a trigger of some kind for us to leave our comfort zone. It's not enough to create a product or service. You also have to create an incentive for customers to buy it.

Marketing and sales initiatives aim to influence customers' behaviour, but behaviour can also be affected by changes in the macro environment. The global financial crisis of 2008 and the pandemic of 2020-22 are examples of major changes to the macro environment. In these environments, customers' attitudes and needs can change quickly and this provides an opportunity for businesses to serve these needs. Some of the best companies were founded in the aftermath of a crisis.

It's in our nature to see a crisis as a threat. Paradoxically, a crisis is as much an opportunity as it is a threat, and a growth mindset would look for opportunities that are made available through the crisis.

Let's get into each of these three themes in more detail.

Chapter 1 - Understanding the problem

A new initiative usually starts with a person and their idea. The idea forms and develops to a point where the will to start is unstoppable.

An entrepreneur will try and imagine every detail of how the business could work. In fact, the ability to imagine how the idea might be brought to life is part of the essence of entrepreneurship.

Then, the idea hits reality. Unless entrepreneurs are careful, they can waste a lot of time and money as they set out to do exactly what they envisioned in the way they imagined it.

> "No battle plan ever survives contact with the enemy." *Prussian Field Marshal Helmuth Karl Bernard Graf von Moltke, 1800-91*

If you have an idea, build a product or service and try to sell it in the way you first imagined, you will probably fail. Much of what you imagined might happen won't happen. Such is life.

A better approach is to put your idea under the microscope and ask yourself, "What am I assuming will be true?" and therefore, "What do I need to test?" From that comes the most important question: "What is the cheapest possible way for me to gather evidence to determine if my assumption is likely to be true or false?"

To start a business, ask questions

There is a logical order in which to test these assumptions.

Start with the assumptions that are closest to the customer:

- What motivates your customers?
- Who are they?
- What is the pain point you are trying to solve?
- Do they care about the pain point?
- Are they willing to pay?
- How much?
- Can you describe your proposition in a way that they will react to it?
- How can you reach these customers?

I recall a networking event where I spoke with founders who had already built a product but who could not answer the questions above. Sometimes it was because they were solving a problem that they faced personally and which they assumed the rest of the world would also want solved (sometimes true, sometimes not). Others had a passion for technology and had built some cool tech without really understanding how to take it to market. Both of these situations made me feel uneasy. I always want to start with the customer and user first.

(By the way, a customer is a person who pays you, and a user is a person who uses the product. Sometimes they're different, such as with Facebook.)

I would urge any entrepreneur starting out to ask first, "What am I trying to prove?"

Break this down into stages:

1. Prove that the problem exists.
2. Prove that there are customers who care.
3. Prove that you have a proposition and message that responds to the demand.
4. Prove that you can deliver a service or product that they want to buy.
5. Prove how you can reach your customers economically.
6. Prove what overheads are needed to service your customers.
7. Prove that your unit economics work.
8. Prove that your partnerships and sales models can work.
9. Prove that you can retain and grow customers.

These are just a taster of some of the questions to ask - the headlines.

Under each can be further detail. Depending on the business model, there will be additional questions to ask.

If I meet an entrepreneur with a bold vision and they can explain to me what their assumptions are and how they will test them, I have more certainty that they will succeed.

The important question therefore is: what do you need to prove first to know that your idea has potential?

Your opinion of your business does not matter

As an investor, I was often asked for my opinion on a business idea.

The truth is, my opinion actually doesn't really matter.

My opinion is not going to be the reason why a venture succeeds or fails. My opinion is just that, an opinion. In the grand scheme of things, it's irrelevant.

> "Your opinion, although interesting, is irrelevant."

I first heard this useful reminder from the team at Pragmatic Marketing. It serves to emphasise that you cannot validate a business idea through the opinion of the creator or investor. Only customers can validate ideas.

In Marc Ecko's excellent book, *Unlabel: Selling You Without Selling Out*, he takes us on a roller-coaster ride through his journey as an entrepreneur, investor and fashion designer - he has packed in a lot since he started out in 1972.

In his own journey he distinguished between gatekeepers and goalkeepers:

> "In our culture, it is too often governed externally, by outside gatekeepers in our lives or industries. Those gatekeepers may indeed formally be that certifying body, an investor or a boss, an influential person or just those cool kids that will roll their eyes at you for even having dared tried. They will get in your way, but those *gatekeepers* are not the *goalkeepers*."

Goalkeepers are your customers. Goalkeepers are the buyers, the people on the street who will use/buy your product and who - if you do it right - will tell others about your product. The opinion of goalkeepers is what really matters.

So, when someone pitched an idea to me (as an investor, a gatekeeper), what I was really looking for was evidence that they had found a deep customer need. That customer need may not have been validated by my opinion - after all, I was probably not the customer (the goalkeeper). I was looking for the entrepreneur to share research results or evidence which showed that buyers liked the idea.

I could ask probing questions and help the entrepreneur think about how to take advantage of the customer need, but I couldn't create the customer need, nor could I validate it.

If you have a business growth idea, your own personal enthusiasm and belief need to be grounded in a real customer need.

What customers value is not what you think they value

This process of customer discovery can yield great insights and provide a strong foundation for an amazing business.

Only if you do it.

Often, I find that it's only in retrospect that entrepreneurs realise just how valuable this interaction is.

The purpose of the discussion is not just to uncover customer behaviours. It's also to ask "why?" and uncover their motivations. Customers' motivations - the layer behind their behaviour - are where the real insight lies. Always ask why.

Motivation may come from a need, a desire, a want, a belief, a habit, a desired identity, a feeling or a drive. We often give ourselves and others a rational reason for why we bought something, but most of the time it was an emotional reason dressed up as a rational reason. Do you really need the latest smartphone? Or do you think it will improve what people think of you?

Here are three examples from my own journey of how conversations with customers led to insights that helped shape product direction.

1. Ski holidays

My first job in the online world was in 2000 when I took a job as a product manager for a website called *ifyouski.com*.

I had spent the previous few years working for a specialist ski chalet tour operator, Simply Ski. It being a small company, we all helped out with manning the phones, and so I spent a couple of summers taking phone enquiries from potential customers.

Each phone call would inevitably start with a conversation where the customer would tell me what they were looking for. It could be a particular chalet from our brochure on a particular date or it could be a more general enquiry. For example, "I'm looking for a chalet for 10 people with childcare, ideally in Val d'Isere or Tignes at Easter, flying from Manchester."

If I didn't have an exact match on this request, I would ask more questions. Why Val d'Isere or Tignes? Would Birmingham be OK if Manchester was unavailable? How many families were travelling? Did they need en-suite facilities? Could they go either of the Easter weeks or just a particular one? And so on. By probing deep into the needs beyond those stated, I could usually find a match for them and suggest a holiday that would suit them.

What people say they want and what they actually need are sometimes different.

Every booker had specific needs. So, at ifyouski.com this learning was baked into the product from day one. If we presented a chalet that matched your dates, we would also tell you on which other dates it might be available. We provided a way to browse chalets by date, by resort and by discount. We allowed people to filter on chalet size, airport, childcare, self-catering versus catered, and so on.

We made sure the online search reflected the way people searched offline.

2. Online booking for restaurants

In 2009 at Livebookings (later known as Bookatable), we were leading the way in Europe with online booking systems for restaurants.

We were looking at our product strategy and, as COO, I knew that I needed to understand our customers better. Together with our product manager, Jay, we visited 12 different restaurants in a month. We spent 30 to 60 minutes at each, interviewing marketing managers, operational managers and general managers about how they marketed and ran their restaurants and their attitudes to online booking.

A clear insight that came from these meetings was around pricing. We used to price our service on a per diner basis. It was 75p per diner for bookings from a restaurant's own website and £2 per diner for bookings through our network of partners.

I remember a restaurant's marketing manager explaining to me that she had a fixed marketing budget for the year. Our fees came out of her budget. The more bookings we did, the less money she had to spend on anything else, including things such as Christmas menu cards.

We pointed out we were bringing in customers that she would not have otherwise had and that this could be seen as a positive return on investment with no risk on her spend. All very well, she noted, but it didn't mean the restaurant owner would give her a bigger marketing budget.

What she needed was predictability.

It turns out we had been wrong that people wanted a pure pay-for-performance model. Rationally, we thought pay-for-performance offered the best value for customers, but they didn't see it that way. Irrationally, they wanted to pay more for predictability.

After that we changed our pricing. We went from a pay-as-you-go model to an "all-you-can-eat" one, allowing her an unlimited number of bookings through her own website for a higher fixed fee per month.

3. Holiday rentals

When I was COO at the holiday lettings startup *HouseTrip* (since acquired by Tripadvisor), I used to travel to our Lisbon office a lot. In 2012 alone, I was there 26 times.

On each trip I would book a different rental through the HouseTrip website. I used our website as a consumer would, noting small things that had improved or identifying ways in which we could improve further.

Importantly though, on every visit I would have a chance to meet with one of the apartment owners and find out more about them.

One I remember clearly was Olivier, who had three apartments that he ran as a small business in his spare time (he had a day-job as well). Olivier had tried different websites to market his properties and had an opinion on each of them, including ours. In one 30-minute conversation I learned a lot.

Olivier was paying €450 a year to a competitor to list his property (even though on our website he listed for free). That was because on the competitor website, customers had left reviews on his (excellent) property and service. If he stopped paying the listing fees, he would lose this excellent content.

He valued positive reviews.

We were new to the market and hadn't yet sent him enough bookings to build a solid review base. (Later we would send him more bookings than anyone else.) I realised that having lots of positive reviews would not only help consumers to book (I knew that already) but would also help us keep our best owners on the site.

A product team was tasked with finding ways to maximise the number of reviews we collected. Review count became a key performance indicator (KPI) and we gave priority to properties with positive reviews.

Talking with customers is not just for idea-stage entrepreneurs. It's an essential discipline at all stages of company growth. You can always learn more by talking with customers.

Plus, talking with customers is not just important for CEOs and product managers - everyone on the team can learn from it. The shared understanding that this brings can be very powerful.

To grow online bookings, make offline bookings

What has the telephone got to do with online growth?

It can be an important way to prove value early.

My experience in this space was shaped by my time at venture capital firm Forward Partners, where we partnered with several entrepreneurs to develop marketplace businesses. Examples included Appear Here (pop-up shops), Snaptrip (last-minute holiday rentals) and Lexoo (legal services for SMEs).

In all cases, the telephone was an important part of how the startup grew and built great product.

An online marketplace is a website that connects buyers of a service or product with sellers. Appear Here's buyers were retailers who were looking for a short-term rental. Its sellers were landlords. Snaptrip's buyers were holidaymakers. Its sellers were holiday homeowners and letting agents. Lexoo's buyers were small businesses that needed legal help. Its sellers were lawyers. In each case the marketplace made money by taking a small share of the transaction.

Marketplaces work when you have lots of demand (buyers) and lots of supply (sellers). As a buyer, you seek out a place where you can get good choice and good prices. As a seller, you seek out a place where there are lots of buyers. When this is going well, you have what's known as great liquidity (there's a large flow of supply and demand).

It is difficult to build liquidity. You need to find ways to stimulate both supply and demand. In the meantime, you need to build a website/platform where both parties interact. Yet as most startups have very few resources in their first few months, they need to find a way to get started without building all the functionality of a fully developed website.

One technique we encouraged companies to use at this stage involved starting with a very simple website where the aim is to get consumers (buyers) to make a request to buy. This request came in the form of filling out a form and hitting "send", which generated an email to the startup team.

This is where the phone came in. The team phoned the buyer to double check what they needed and why, and then they called the seller to make the purchase/booking/order.

It was a highly manual process and it doesn't scale. Why would a startup do that? Isn't the whole point of a tech startup to develop tech solutions?

The reason is simple: this manual process gives founders a chance to have conversations with real customers. Every interaction is a chance to learn. It provides insight into the motivations of buyers and sellers and helps inform what the product will need to do to delight both.

We called this technique the Concierge MVP (MVP = minimum viable product). Its purpose was to maximise learning and to minimise the risk of building a product that no-one needs or wants.

I'd encourage anyone starting out in business to first solve a problem without technology, and develop deep customer understanding before committing to creating code. Startups always need to hustle and hack to get started. If you're starting a marketplace, I strongly recommend the phone hack. You'll learn a lot and you'll build a great product the first time around.

To solve a problem, don't focus on the solution

"If I had only one hour to save the world, I would spend 55 minutes defining the problem, and only five minutes finding the solution."
Albert Einstein (allegedly)

In meetings where entrepreneurs were pitching to us for investment, the solution (the product) was often explained first. I was trying to make sense of this solution without much information on what is surely the most important part of the equation: the problem.

If I understood the problem better, I'd have a much better chance of deciding whether the solution made sense.

You can briefly explain the solution to provide context and an introduction, but before getting into too much detail, it's important to make sure that the problem is explained properly.

Therefore, my advice to anyone pitching for support or investment is:

- First make sure you've properly understood your customers' needs.
- Then explain the need you are going to meet.

Explain why your customers behave the way they do.

- Show you understand both the rational and emotional drivers of their behaviour.
- Explain who has this need.
- Describe the size of the problem in terms of how many people have this need.
- Explain how you know all of this to be true.
- Then, and only then, pitch the details of your solution.

Your opinion of the solution should depend on your understanding of the problem.

Create a great product by building very little product

"We're going to launch in two months' time, get some early feedback on our idea and then we've a version 2 planned soon after that which does X, Y and Z." *As said by many founders over the years!*

You have an idea. You test the idea by building it. What's wrong with that? It is admittedly one way to test an idea. This approach can sometimes work

- if the idea was right in the first place.

However, it's an expensive way to find out you were wrong. Not only that, but you are also testing a limited and fixed set of features.

A better and cheaper approach is to spend this time first really understanding your customers. Why are you building what you are building in the first place?

- How do your potential customers currently address the need or problem that you want to solve?
- What friction is there in this process?
- What is their motivation for wanting this solved?
- What do they really care about?
- Are they bothered enough to try out alternatives?
- Who are they influenced by and how?

At the beginning of a project, it's wise to build as little product (your prototype) as possible. Only build the full version of your product once you've developed a strong understanding of your customers. The same could be said for buying or holding inventory in the example of a business stocking physical goods.

The paradox here is that the less you build, the more likely you are to succeed.

Of course, at some point you do need to launch a product and the purpose of doing so is to test if customers respond to the proposition. Before doing so, there's a lot that can be tested without building anything. Customer discovery can yield lots of useful information. Customer discovery doesn't just involve interviewing customers. It can also include statistical research, building prototypes and seeing how customers interact with them. The purpose of customer discovery is to validate the idea and refine the proposition. It can turn an OK idea into a great idea. Plus, it's far cheaper.

On customer discovery, if there is one book to read for someone looking to create a business, it's Rob Fitzpatrick's *The Mom Test*. Rob explains:

> "People say you shouldn't ask your mom whether your business is a good idea. That's true, but it misses the point. You shouldn't ask anyone whether your business is a good idea. At least not in those words. Admittedly, your mom will lie to you the most (weird, right?). But everyone will lie to you at least a little. Ultimately it's a bad question, and it's not their responsibility to show us the truth. It's our responsibility to find it. We do that by asking good questions."

Rob's book helps you to ask the right questions. Please read it.

Moonshots start on the ground

T-minus 10 seconds and counting. Five, four, three, two, one - we have lift off!

Once you have identified a customer need and you have an idea of a product you can build or sell to fulfill it, you can start the difficult job of launching a business.

The bigger the rocket, the more difficult it is to launch. So to get off the ground, reduce the size of your rocket.

It may well be that your amazing business idea could eventually be sold to a huge number of people in a huge number of ways, through many channels and in many places. It's true that big successful businesses do exactly that. But small ones don't. Small businesses get going by being focussed, creating early success and then building on that success. The same goes for new projects within established businesses.

Your plan for getting to the moon must start with first getting off the ground. And for that you need three ingredients:

1. A target customer segment.
2. A product or service that solves a need.
3. A sales and marketing channel to reach your customers.

Your first milestone of success is to find a combination of these three things that work for you.

Once you find this trinity that gets you moving, your business initiative will leave the ground and be on its way. When you're ready, you can add to this mix. You could add an additional product and sell it to the same customers through the same channels. You could add an additional customer segment that you sell your existing product to. Or you could find new sales channels. Just don't try to do all three at the same time.

Say you are selling baseball caps online (product) to UK sports fans (segment) via social media ads (channel). Once you've got that working, you could try adding sports team shirts (additional product) to the mix. If that works, you could start targeting parents looking for birthday gifts (additional segment). If that works, you could develop paid search advertising (additional channel). Imagine making the pyramid wider and wider once you have a good foundation.

If you try to sell multiple products to multiple segments through multiple channels all at once, you have a greater chance of failure. You will have higher overheads and bigger risks. The one channel, one product, one segment approach is less risky and carries fewer overheads. Your early successes can help fund investment in your subsequent growth experiments.

You don't just launch a rocket ship and go straight to Mars. You have to first work out how to get off the ground. Paradoxically, those that succeed with their moonshots don't focus on the moon - they focus on getting off the ground.

Chapter 2 - Reducing friction

With a problem to solve, how can it be solved better? Reduce friction. Making something easy is really at the heart of business growth. Easy for customers, easy for the team, easy for partners, easy for suppliers.

Easy creates value. Easy to make choices, easy to pay, easy to use, easy to find, easy to secure, easy to process, easy to contact, easy to fix, easy to build.

There may well be other ways to create value but I honestly believe that reducing friction is at the heart of growth.

Helping others to win will help you win

As a teenager I couldn't quite get my head around business terminology. Words like operations, marketing, supply chain and procurement meant nothing to me. It seemed that business was complicated. My mum was a pharmacist and my dad was an electrical engineer. I could understand what they did but no-one really explained how companies worked.

I thought about doing Business Studies at university but couldn't get excited enough to choose to study it (it all seemed very abstract) and ironically instead chose Theology and Religious Studies (abstract?). This involved a lot of human questions. We studied different religions, ethics, sociology and philosophy. Admittedly, this might seem equally complicated to some people, but for me it was a good fit.

Since then I've understood how businesses work by being part of them. I do now understand most of those previously complex terms.

After 35 years of working, the penny has dropped. Business can *seem* complicated. It doesn't have to be. I believe that good business - in its purest form - is about helping people.

The paradox is that if you want to win, you do it by first helping others to win. Altruism beats ego every time.

A few examples of how different types of businesses help:

- Farmers help people by providing food for them to eat.
- Telephone manufacturers help people communicate easily.
- Airlines help people visit friends and family.
- Recruiters help companies find people to join their teams.
- Investors help entrepreneurs get their businesses going.
- Lego and Minecraft help children develop creative skills.

Companies that are successful in helping people can grow fast. As companies scale and grow, we humans use a great trick to get things done: division of labour. We all have different skills. Those of us who are good with numbers might take finance, those who are good at persuading people might do sales. Organised people might do operations, and those with empathy work in customer service.

This method has many benefits, efficiency being one of them. We're all different and can work with our strengths. It's a very logical thing to do but it has side effects that we need to be aware of.

If roles are divided, fewer people talk directly with customers, the people we are helping. This is a problem because it's only when you truly understand your customers that you can help them properly.

Organise around your customer

A new generation of companies are finding ways to keep their teams directly in contact with their customers. Many are covered in Frédéric Laloux's 2014 book, *Reinventing Organizations*. One example given is *Buurtzorg*, a home-care nursing company in the Netherlands that has thousands of nurses working in small self-managed teams deciding on how best to serve its customers.

Remove abstraction and reduce friction

It's my view that while division of labour is useful to a point, it creates abstraction - i.e. it distances us from our customers. Organisations with increased division of labour end up with decreased customer empathy, and it becomes more difficult to provide meaning to customers and employees.

I'm not saying we shouldn't have specialised roles. Not at all. We need specialised skills. What I'm saying is that we need to avoid creating specialisation when none is needed.

We also may need to focus on initiatives to increase customer knowledge and awareness in non-customer-facing teams.

As humans, we are social animals designed to succeed by helping each other.

To delight your customer, be your customer

It's only when you actually experience being a customer that you really know what it is you are selling. OK, you might be able to hold the product you are selling. You might be able to go into the shop and see the shop. It's not until you actually try and find the shop for the first time, find what you are looking for, buy it and take it home to use it that you truly experience what you are offering your customer.

The key point is this: you never sell a product - you always sell an experience.

Let's take an example: the iPod. The iPod was phenomenally successful. People extolled the virtues of the user interface, the design, the packaging, the marketing.

Really though, it's the sum of all of these parts (and more) that made the iPod a breakthrough experience. The marketing campaigns conveyed a simplicity and cool factor. If you were to buy one from an Apple store (online or in the high street), you would be wowed by state-of-the-art presentation. You would get good service in the shop or, if online, you'd get a website that was well designed and easy to buy from. The packaging was so slick, neat and clean. You unwrapped your iPod and it just felt great. You'd just plug it into your computer, it charged fast. You downloaded iTunes - nice and easy. In fact, iTunes was just as much a part of the iPod experience as the player itself. It was all so easy. Then of course, there was the user interface - the simple controls. On top of that, it just looked cool.

Since then, technology has moved on. Streaming, earbuds, superfast Wi-Fi. At the time though, in the mid-noughties, Apple absolutely delivered on great experience.

You see, the iPod was not successful for any one of these individual factors. The total experience is what counts.

For any business, therefore, every point of detail matters. The message, the communication, the product features, the sales process, the purchase experience, the convenience, delivery/pick up experience, customer service, product reliability. None of these details ever stand alone.

Unless you are a company of just one person, you always have different staff members dealing with different parts of the experience. As a result, none of them get to see the overall picture from a customer's perspective.

The only way to see what you are really delivering is to be your own customer.

Go and buy your own product. See what it feels like. Is it good enough? Is it better than that of your competitors? Go and test their products too. Now you're getting somewhere.

You don't build product, you build an experience

Just as you never sell a product (you always sell an experience), you don't build a product - you build an experience.

You're sitting in a restaurant having a great time. In fact, it's a wonderful evening. You have a good round table with a bunch of friends, the food is fantastic, the service is excellent and the wine is flowing. The next day, you get an email from the restaurant owner asking you to rate your visit. You give it five stars. It was fantastic.

Mrs Restaurant Owner was very happy because her customer was deeply satisfied with the experience. She also runs a good business, so she made some money that night. Overall, it was a success for everyone involved. Fantastic guest experience, good business, everyone is happy. Wonderful. Beautiful. Perfect.

Ah. Experience. That's a troublesome thing, you see, because it's actually quite difficult to establish what precisely it was about the experience that was good. Was it the conversation? Was it the company? Both of these things? Or the food? Or the seating configuration? In fact, it's all of these and much more. Experience is an emerging phenomenon. Getting a specific individual to feel, well, something emerges through a complex interplay of events, relationships, objects and timing.

Product managers of a website have the same challenge as restaurant owners. They need to create an emergent set of experiences that support the business objectives. Those emergent experiences could be for example, ease of use, joy, engagement, desire, advocacy (telling others), typing in credit card numbers, or creating a profile.

A product manager therefore is the custodian of experience.

Creating something which emerges from many factors is bloody difficult. However, if something is difficult to do, it's difficult for others to copy, so it's worth doing. And creating emergent systems that create wonderful experiences is extremely difficult. It's part art and part science.

In this intangible sphere of experience, first you need to understand the systems from which your experience will come. The restaurant owner looks at all the details, from the hiring of chefs, the organisation of the kitchen and the buying of ingredients to menu design, staffing rotas and hundreds of other small details, and tries to create repeatable patterns of success that result in the experiences that restaurant goers rave about. It's difficult in a restaurant and it's difficult on a website or app.

This web of interrelated influences that creates emergent behaviour works a little like the human brain itself, in which a network of synapses fires messages from one node to another to create a state of awareness at any single moment. Time adds a further dimension, because each customer interacts with your company several times in several ways in different states of mind at different locations.

A creative product manager will first try to understand the web of influences, understand the triggers and amplify the ones that work, as well as trying new things that could be new influences and triggers. All the time, they will be measuring the impact as best they can.

Here's the thing though - experience can never be fully measured. The very thing that you are trying to create is elusive and ephemeral.

You can measure many aspects of experience, many dimensions. Snapshots. Like the restaurant rating from the delighted customer. You cannot really feel the experience of others, but you need to do your damn best to try. One thing you can do however is to wear your customers' shoes. Buy from your own company as a customer would. Experience the marketing, the packaging, the product, the app and so on. Your own experience is the experience of one, but it is very real. Your own experience is not elusive or ephemeral, it's raw, real and valid.

If you are a product manager, you are dealing with millions of those experiences. And furthermore, you are building an interface that your customer will experience using a team of other people. So you are building great experiences for others, through others. This is an incredibly tough but rewarding challenge. Paradoxically, you are not actually managing a product. You are engineering experience. Maybe you should have the job title of "experience engineer".

Look to your customers for your failures, not your successes

The zombie question. It's a great question. I promise.

In the zombie movie *World War Z* (with Brad Pitt), there's a scene in which the zombies are trying to breach the city walls in Jerusalem. Zombies are scrambling over each other in a huge, frenzied pile to try to get through, but only a handful succeed at first.

This reminded me that sometimes online companies have an amazing offering but so often customers have big walls to climb to get to the feast.

A prospect makes their way all the way through the user journey and becomes a customer. They transact. Wow, result! The product works. Maybe they signed up for a paid subscription, bought some goods, requested a quote, became a member of your network or paid for an in-app purchase.

They made it. They made it through an obstacle course to pay you some money. Result!

These are your early adopters. They know they have a pain and they are looking for medicine to ease it. They are the easiest customers to convert. If you've read Geoffrey Moore, you'll know there is a chasm to cross so that your product sells not just to the early adopters but to the early majority as well.

For a product or service to become a lasting success, it needs to appeal not only to the early adopters but also to the early majority.

You'll want to find out where these early majority customers are having problems with your product and try to fix them. The problem you have is that because they didn't become customers, you don't have their contact details to ask them.

You can however ask the people who did make it through - your first customers, the early adopters.

So here's the question. Ask your early adopters this:

"What's the one thing that nearly stopped you buying from us?"

This is a great question. It tells you what were the main things that held them back. Ideally ask this question over the telephone or face to face if you can. You'll get a better flavour of the issues they had than if you ask them over email or other digital channels.

The answers to this question will reveal obstacles. It could be your returns policy, it could be not being able to find said policy soon enough, or it could be even something more subtle - something emotional such as "I've never heard of these guys. Do I trust them?"

Think of these obstacles like large walls in your product which the early adopters managed to climb over. Stacked up behind those walls are the bodies of the early majority. They'd be your customers too in a flash if you could lower or remove those walls.

Use analytics to observe what's happening on that page. Use session tracking video if you can. Target these obstacles in usability testing and identify things you think you can improve to break them down.

With these insights you can then systematically build hypotheses to test to see if your changes reduce the obstacles and improve the product.

I am not advocating that companies think of their customers as the undead. Quite the opposite in fact. Customers are the lifeblood of any business. Just to be clear.

In any system you get out what you put in

Online marketplaces are systems that bring together buyers and sellers. The sellers are varied and have different products. Bringing all of this product together on one platform is how a marketplace provides choice for consumers.

One often overlooked yet important driver of marketplace success is what I call the standardisation of the presentation of supply. In a world of infinite variety, make the most of that variety by having a standard way of presenting the goods or services available to sell.

Range of choice and tools to navigate that choice

By supply, I mean whatever is being sold on the marketplace. You could call it the product catalogue or the inventory. Whatever you call it, a good marketplace helps buyers to search, filter and compare the choices available to them.

For example, if I search for hotels in Central London on Booking.com I get thousands of hotels returned. I can filter my choices down to ones that might suit me better (e.g. I only want three-star hotels with Wi-Fi, air conditioning and family rooms, and where the reviews are better than 8/10). With filters, I can now find something to meet my needs.

Being able to search and filter is what customers need to make sense of so much choice.

Good UI is a growth driver

User interface (UI) design determines how easy it is for buyers to find what they are looking for.

In a real-world store such as a supermarket, goods are categorised and arranged into sections (dairy, bakery, fruit and vegetables etc.). Likewise, online marketplaces need to organise their goods. Search and filter is the cornerstone user interface design for online marketplaces.

And when you've found a couple of things that interest you, you might want to compare choices. If product listings have some consistency in their presentation, you can compare options more easily. It's not just about how you find products; it's about how you present them. UK online estate agent Rightmove does this well. Each listing has a consistent layout, giving some predictability to the user experience.

If search, filter and compare are done well, the conversion rate from visitor to buyer is improved. The better the conversion rate, the more the marketplace can afford to pay to acquire customers (i.e. a bigger marketing budget). A bigger marketing budget drives growth and growth drives market share.

As a marketplace, you want to be number one in your sector. (After all, buyers search eBay because there is so much choice, and sellers list on eBay because there are so many buyers.)

One of the foundations of growth therefore is making it super easy for customers to find what they want.

Good UI needs standardisation of datasets

1. Search, filter and compare requires that software can compare like-for-like data to find matches and mismatches. If Booking.com wants to offer a filter choice such as Wi-Fi, every hotel needs a Y/N flag in the database on whether it has Wi-Fi.

This means that every product listing needs to store as much information as possible in a standard data format. It's difficult to write code to compare two hotel descriptions if they are just text. If some of the attributes of the hotel are stored as data points that the code can compare, you can use these comparisons in search and filter.

A key component therefore of marketplace success is the ability to create a standard data structure to normalise what would otherwise be a disparate set of product listings.

Good data sets need good data frameworks and collection processes

Standardisation is important for most marketplaces. For marketplaces where sellers can list their own products directly (e.g. eBay), it's particularly important to build input forms that collect the data in a structured way. If you use the eBay iPhone app to list an item for sale, you'll notice just how much standardisation has been designed into the data structure - right down to the postage choices.

The information architecture of a product listing is therefore a critical part of the product/service design and is often overlooked. Getting this right early can help a marketplace give a better consumer experience.

When building a marketplace, a key priority in the product design process is mapping out the data structures for each listing type. The question to ask is "Does this information have to be in words?"

Other data formats that are more comparable include:

- Yes/no
- Date
- Number
- Choices from a predefined list.

This type of data is structured data. Build listings on structured data and you will be able to build great product discovery tools and achieve listing presentation that is consistently high quality.

Curated versus non-curated marketplaces

A curated marketplace is where the marketplace chooses which merchants or suppliers to feature. A non-curated marketplace is where anyone can list. Booking.com is an example of a curated marketplace; eBay is a non-curated marketplace.

Non-curated marketplaces face the greatest challenge in maintaining standardisation in terms of how supply is presented. It is normally done by allowing suppliers relatively little freedom in how listings are added. You need to adhere to a specific format. Product managers in such marketplaces give a lot of attention to validating the inputs from suppliers into their systems. Form design, validation scripts, application programming interfaces (API) and spreadsheet import structures will, if all done well, have a strong positive influence on the quality and consistency of inventory data.

Curated marketplaces can afford to have fewer systems to control the data input process - provided they have human beings to do the quality checking or content loading. Sometimes the same rigour is needed with input forms, but these might be internal systems rather than externally facing systems.

If data quality is important, how do we improve it?

Quality control

An important operational activity for a marketplace is quality control. A person or team is tasked with analysing the integrity of the data and making plans to improve it.

I've found that a good starting place to analyse the quality of listings is to produce exception reports. These tell you which of your listings/products don't match the criteria/standards you are looking for. For example, if you require at least three photos per product, you need a simple report that shows you any product that has fewer than three photos. It doesn't need to be a fancy web reporting system; it could simply be a query against your database and a text file report.

By finding exceptions and then systematically correcting them, you can improve the overall data quality. Then it's important to give feedback to the product team so they can improve the data entry points to prevent the exceptions from occurring again.

Good data only gets you so far

It's not all about structured data though - there needs to be a wow in the product that brings people back.

For example, this could include:

- Great inspirational design
- Curated showrooms that help visitors discover exciting goods
- Amazing price promotions
- Superb photography
- Expert reviews
- User-generated reviews
- Simple payment and delivery options

However, my point remains this: structured datasets are essential to get right when building great marketplaces.

Chapter 3 - Change behaviour

Can you paint a picture of the future you are trying to build? In, say, three years' time, who will be your customers, what will they buy, how will they buy it and what experience of your company will they have? If you have found a way to reduce friction and create value, can you think ahead to what that might mean for your customers, your team and your business?

Great companies change their customers and great customers change companies

I've always been a fan of the definition of a startup given by entrepreneur and academic Steve Blank:

> "A startup is an organisation formed to search for a repeatable and scalable business model."

I'd like to offer an extension of that excellent definition:

The purpose of a startup is to change behaviour.

I say this because any startup needs to find a way to disrupt existing behaviours and create a business where customers pay, suppliers are happy, the team enjoy working there and investors want to put money in to grow the business.

- Change the behaviour of potential customers.
- Change the behaviour of potential suppliers.
- Change the behaviour of potential investors.
- Change the behaviour of team members.

When you start thinking of creating a business in this way, it becomes apparent that entrepreneurs are agents of change.

Paradoxically, people who start businesses are not really starting businesses - they are creating a movement which will change the behaviour of many people. All being well, that movement will become a viable business in due course.

Rational and emotional

These startup challenges require an understanding of not only the rational reasons why people currently do things but also their emotional reasons.

One of the most powerful things an entrepreneur can do is think about why. Why do people behave the way they do? Why would they care? Why will they change? Why, why, why?

Rational reasons are not enough. "Buy this product because it is better" is not usually enough to persuade people to buy. Successful entrepreneurs tap into their feelings, motivations and identities.

For example, some people buy airport parking because they don't want to rely on anyone else to get to the airport. They don't want to rely on public transport and they don't want to rely on a taxi turning up. They want control. This is a powerful emotion. You can position your product or service with rational reasons (e.g. it's cheaper to book in advance), but for some customers a stronger message would be emotional (e.g. take yourself on holiday, on time, every time).

The reasons why people do things are deep and varied. Understanding these reasons is the secret of unlocking potential growth. It shapes product design, messaging and the go-to-market plan.

Change behaviours and change the world

Here are a few examples of how companies have changed my own behaviour:

- I used to pay with a debit card, I now pay with my phone.
- I used not to stop for coffee on my way to work, I now do it daily.
- I used to pre-book a taxi, now I just request one from an app.
- I used to take a tent with me on holiday, now I can book one that is already set up.
- I used to go to the supermarket every week, I now have my groceries delivered.

Not only have the companies behind these changes found a repeatable business model, but they have done so by successfully changing the behaviour of people like me and you.

Being fit for purpose is never fit for purpose

In the early 2000s, entrepreneurs Steve Blank and Eric Ries coined the term "lean startup". Lean startup is a methodology for approaching the creation of new businesses. It is based upon principles, one of which is the "build, measure, learn" cycle.

Thanks to Eric Ries, Steve Blank and the whole lean startup movement, increasing numbers of founders and investors are more aware of the need for quickly validating that a new business has a "product-market fit".

Rob Fitzpatrick (author of *The Mom Test*) reminded me that there are three words in that phrase and that each word matters.

Product fit, market fit and product-market fit are each worth understanding in their own right. As a founder or investor, it's worth knowing the difference and which matters to your business.

An emphasis on product fit is most important when the market is already understood. For example, when we know that people want to play games online, the important thing is to work on building a great game. Product fit.

An emphasis on market fit is important when the customers' needs are not yet understood fully. For example, if a startup were to focus on improving tools for events and event organisers, it would need to understand the current pain points and identify something real and tangible that it can improve and for which people are willing to pay. Market fit.

Product-market fit brings product fit and market fit together.

Product-market fit means that i) the problem exists, ii) the solution solves the problem, and iii) customers are willing to pay for the solution.

Depending on the opportunity being explored, it may be that a deeper understanding of the market is first needed. In other cases, the market needs could be already well understood and the key question is whether the proposed product is a good solution for those market needs.

The most relevant word of all is fit. Any business that succeeds needs to be fit for purpose. This fitness relates to being adapted to the current and future environment. It's precisely the fact that the environment in which we find ourselves is constantly changing (technological trends, social trends, legislative changes etc.) that gives businesses new opportunities to exploit. It also means that all businesses, large or small, need to continuously adapt to make sure that their product meets the needs of customers.

Just as an athlete can train to be fit for a certain event, a business needs to be fit to exploit their opportunity. Usually a training schedule for boxing won't help you win a swimming race. Training to run a marathon won't help you win the 100m sprint.

In the earliest phase of a business, research therefore needs to focus on defining the opportunity and figuring out what's needed to win that opportunity. Then it's time to get fit.

As soon as you have "fit", you'll lose it. The market, your customers' needs and technology all change day by day. Getting fit is hard. Staying fit is just as hard.

Your vision is not a strategy

What is a vision and why is it different from a strategy?

A vision focuses on tomorrow and describes what an organisation wants to ultimately become. A strategy focuses on today and what an organisation does to achieve the vision. Both vision and strategy are vital in directing goals.

Vision? Mission? Purpose? Strategy? Objectives? Goals? You could be forgiven for getting these mixed up and you'd be surprised at how many people do. I'll explain more in the next section. However, it's very simple. If you distill all of the above to the absolute basics, it's as simple as saying "Do X in order to achieve Y", where X is the strategy and plan and Y is the vision.

It doesn't have to be complicated. Whether you are referring to a team, a company or your life, being able to describe both the vision and the strategy in clear terms is essential to make progress against goals. What's important is that you know at the very minimum i) what you want to become and ii) what you need to do to make it happen. This is the foundation for aligning teams into a common direction.

Let's look at a couple of examples.

Amazon has a vision: "Amazon strives to be Earth's most customer-centric company, Earth's best employer, and Earth's safest place to work."

How will it do that? It will "continually raise the bar of the customer experience by using the internet and technology to help consumers find, discover and buy anything, and empower businesses and content creators to maximise their success."

It's an X (raise the bar...) in order to be Y (...most customer-centric...).

Southwest Airlines? Do X ("connect people to what's important in their lives through friendly, reliable, and low-cost air travel") to achieve Y ("be the world's most loved, most efficient, and most profitable airline").

In both examples, there will be a whole level of detail that goes into the strategy (the larger plan will include objectives, time frames, measures and resources) but you can see that Amazon is doubling down on customer experience through technology and Southwest is focussed on low cost with great service.

Building out the detail around the strategy will involve lots of initiatives around areas each company is looking to improve or change, expressed as objectives. Each objective will serve their high-level strategy to achieve their vision. Each objective will have measures around it to assess the impact.

If the company or organisation does this well, each team should be able to relate what they are doing to the wider strategy and see how it helps them achieve the vision.

Even on a day-to-day basis, I find "Do X in order to achieve Y" a useful framework. If ever I'm presented with an X without a Y (a strategy without a vision), I want to know what Y is. Vice versa, if I am presented with a Y without an X (a vision without a strategy), I need to know what X is. You always need both X and Y. They are cornerstones of understanding against which you can set goals and measure progress.

Strategy has a foundation in beliefs

Companies talk of purpose, vision, mission, strategy, objectives and goals. At first, I found all of this very confusing. The words seemed to be used interchangeably and I needed to be very clear on what they all meant before I could make sense of how to use them.

I now understand. So in the hope of helping others on their own growth journey, here are the definitions I use. I present them in order of time frame, from longer term to shorter term.

Belief

A belief is deeply held, is enduring and provides a strong foundation for everything. The core belief drives purpose (see below); a purpose is based on a belief or set of beliefs.

Purpose

Purpose is long term. It's why. It should be something that could last for decades.

Vision

A vision is medium term. It's a horizon that you are headed for. It's a way of describing what your customers will experience in (say) five years from now.

Strategy

The strategy is the overall plan to get to the vision. It includes goals.

Goals

Goals are long-term ambitions that help achieve the vision. They could be multi-year. A vision can have many goals.

Objectives

These are specific, short-term targets; they are measuring points, or milestones, to help assess progress. A goal can have many objectives.

Deliverables

A deliverable is a specific project to achieve the objective. An objective can have many deliverables.

Here's an example from an imaginary train company:

- Belief: Face-to-face human connection is truly valuable.
- Purpose: Connect friends, family and businesses.
- Vision: Reliable, good-value train travel.
- Mission or strategy: Operational excellence to drive value and reliability.
- Goal 1: Reduce customer impact and cost from train delays.
- Objective 1: Identify root causes of train delays.
- Deliverable a: Collect data on delays into a single repository.

- Deliverable b: Dashboard that identifies top drivers of delays.

Creating and executing on a plan is difficult without having a full stack, from belief to deliverables.

In the past I've been in the situation of having to prioritise multiple projects (objectives and their deliverables) without really knowing the full context of the goals we were aiming to achieve, the vision we were trying to realise or the purpose we were pursuing.

To go faster, to focus on the right deliverables in the right order, requires first standing back and starting with the big questions, such as "What do we believe?", "Why are we here?" and "Where are we headed?" With those clearly stated, prioritisation and organisation of resources can become clearer and more focussed.

Part 1 - question prompts

Before we move on to Part 2, here are some questions you can ask yourself to find your own growth opportunities.

> If you are inexperienced in an area, what questions will you ask to take advantage of your curiosity?

> Do you see uncertainty as a threat or are you looking for the opportunities?

> Do you embrace your fear and do it anyway?

> How can you invest in your personal growth to help your business grow?

> What assumptions can you test and what questions would you ask to test them?

> Do you know what your customers really think, want and need?

> Do you know what your customers are willing to pay for and why?

> Can you think of any hacks to test online processes before you build them by doing them manually first?

> Do you spend your time on understanding the problem or are you rushing to build a solution?

> Can you build less product but invest time in testing it thoroughly and focus on learning?

> Can you think of the first thing you need to do and get started, rather than worrying too much about the master plan?

> Where can you help others to win?

> Have you experienced your company/service/product as a customer does?

> Are you thinking about the whole experience your customer receives and how you can improve it?

> Can you ask your customers what nearly stopped them buying from you and learn from that and improve?

> Can you standardise the way you collect information about your inventory so that it's easier to search?

> How will your customers behave differently as a result of using your product?

> Are you continuously assessing if what you are offering both meets the

needs of your customer and is competitive in the market?

> Have you clearly defined and communicated your vision, and do you have a high-level plan of what you'd need to do to get there? Is this shared and understood?

> Does your plan have some clear objectives and measures of success? Do your team understand these?

3

Part 2: Unlocking growth - Choosing what to do first or next

Chapter 1 - Growth mindset

Once you've validated that a customer need exists and that you can build a product or service to meet it, you'll have lots of work to do to build on the opportunity. Choosing what to do next can seem overwhelming. Here are a few ideas on how you can develop a mindset that will help you progress.

If you can't think backwards from a goal, think forward

There's a large pike swimming in the lily pond. It's hungry and it likes eating frogs. A frog wants to cross the lily pond without being eaten by the pike. So, it jumps from pad to pad.

It helps if it can see the other side of the pond because then it can pick the quickest route across.

If it can't see the other side, it can only cross through trial and error. If it does well, at some point it might see the other side of the pond. At this point it will figure out the final moves to reach the other side.

Depending on whether the frog can see the other side or not, it will have to think either backwards or forwards.

Thinking backwards versus forwards

Thinking backwards means mapping the steps back from the destination and setting in place a plan to follow these steps.

Thinking forwards means asking what the best move to make is, given the information at hand.

Project managers are great at thinking backwards. Starting with a clearly defined end product, they work out what steps are needed in order to get from the present to the end point.

I always wonder how they know what needs to go into the plan. In a tall skyscraper project there must be huge teams of project managers but somehow, they manage to put a plan together with a high degree of accuracy in cost and time. I could say the same for event organisers. Good ones are amazing to watch; they seem to predict the future.

The advantage that project managers for buildings and events have is that a lot (I won't say all) of what is needed to complete the project is predictable because it's been done before.

Startups however can rarely see the other bank of the pond on the day they start. If they think they can, it's probably a hallucination.

There may well be a strong vision of why they are crossing the pond, but it's always a big step into the unknown.

Forward thinking with a purpose

Randomly jumping from one lily pad to another is going to consume a lot of energy.

It would be better to have a clear view on why you are going to try that next lily pad. It's about having a test to know whether that route is going to be interesting.

Recognising assumptions and testing out lots of different hypotheses quickly is the fastest way to discover if the far bank does actually exist and what the best route to get there is.

When I can't see the other bank, I always ask myself, "Given what I now know, what is the best thing to do next and what will I learn by doing so? Is that the smartest move?" It's the only way I've found to make progress in the face of uncertainty.

A good method to navigate the lily pond is to start by mapping out your assumptions using a *lean canvas*. (Search online to find examples.)

Assumptions are either hard to test or easy to test and they are critical or less critical.

On a frequent basis it's helpful to categorise the known assumptions on these two dimensions in a simple 2 x 2 matrix. Then set aside the assumptions that are in the easy-to-test/critical quadrant and prioritise these tests first. That's the first jump to make.

To be a frog is to be human

Human progress is in many ways thanks to our ability to think about the future, imagine what we want it to be like and then take actions to make that future real.

In every project we undertake, big or small, sometimes we know the way, sometimes we don't. Recognising this is an important first step in deciding what type of thinking to deploy.

If the destination is visible and the path is clear, thinking backwards is the best thing to do. Make a step-by-step plan and then deploy it.

If the destination is unclear, it helps to be a forward-thinking frog.

Build the plane before the engine

In 1903, aviation pioneers Wilbur and Orville Wright and Samuel Pierpont Langley embarked on a race to achieve powered flight. Langley, backed by the US government, concentrated on creating a potent engine, believing power was the key to keep an aircraft aloft. His first flight attempt in October, using a substantial 50-horsepower engine, ended in failure. Another attempt two months later was similarly disastrous, leading to public humiliation and criticism for squandering taxpayers' money.

Meanwhile, the Wright brothers adopted a different strategy. They prioritised perfecting balance and steering, choosing to build a glider that would smoothly descend from a hilltop, and focussed less on the engine. After three years, their glider was successful. Collaborating with a bicycle shop engineer, they constructed a lightweight 12-horsepower engine.

Mounting this tiny power source onto their glider, they created their aircraft. On 17 December 1903, the Wright brothers achieved the first successful powered flight in Kitty Hawk, North Carolina, etching their names in history. Meanwhile, Langley, who banked on raw power, has been largely forgotten.

The engine of growth is useless without a good plane. Think of the plane as the product and the engine as marketing.

So many startups start spending money on acquiring customers through marketing before they have a robust product. They have a product that only just works and focus on "traction" quickly because "traction" is what's needed to get the attention of investors.

They spend money to get traction. Without good unit economics, high conversion rates and repeat business, this is like putting a heavy engine in a plane and hoping it will take off. If, however, like the Wright brothers, you build a great product that flies, adding marketing will help it fly faster and further.

It's only when you've got the product right that you should add the marketing engine.

Continuous improvement is relentless

Knowing when good enough is good enough is tricky. You need to get the balance right.

On one hand, there is no such thing as perfect, and performance can always be better. Improvement is a relentless mission. A product can always be better. Service can always be better. I can always be better. Embracing that this is the case helps us set high standards.

In a business context, pausing and saying "That's good enough" may well allow your competitors to move ahead of you. On a personal level, you can get set in your ways. "Good enough" or "That'll do" risk letting entropy take hold. The day you stop trying to improve is the day you start going backwards - because the world around you will move ahead and start leaving you behind. Such is the nature of evolution.

Yet there are plenty of times when saying that something is good enough is exactly the right thing to do. Version 1 of a product need not be perfect if what you are doing is trying to learn quickly. In fact, you might have a better chance of long-term success by releasing something less than perfect to get an early reaction.

(As a side note, that's exactly what I did with this book. My first manuscript was far from perfect, but it was good enough to get a reaction from beta readers and to identify areas for improvement. Ironically, this section is one that I rewrote thanks to that feedback.)

Relentless improvement does not mean waiting for perfection before shipping. It means shipping what you've got, learning what works and what doesn't, and improving based on the feedback. But doing this relentlessly every day is a path to growth - in business and in life, every day, every week, every month and every year.

The catch is that if you obsess about perfection it can cause its own problems. You can lose track of the big picture. You try to win for the sake of winning. It can be toxic and take its toll on your personal and family life.

So the trick is to stand back and take an objective view on i) whether you could improve and ii) whether this is the right thing to focus on right now. This approach allows you to admit improvement is possible but also make a conscious choice about whether to pursue that improvement. The cost or effort of improvement may not be worth it.

There is no such thing as bad luck

An old farmer worked his crops for many years. He had a horse, but it ran away.

His neighbour said, "Such bad luck, I'm so sorry. You must be so upset."

"We'll see," the farmer replied.

A few days later, the horse returned with 10 other wild horses following. The man and his only son rounded up all the horses.

His neighbour said, "Wow, congratulations! How wonderful. You must be so happy!"

The old man replied, "We'll see."

The next day his son tried to ride one of the untamed horses. The horse kicked the man's son, breaking his leg.

His neighbour came to offer his sympathy. "Such bad luck! You must be so upset."

"We'll see," said the farmer.

The country went to war, and military officials toured the villages drafting every able-bodied young man to fight. They spared the son with the broken leg. All the other sons of the village were sent to a bloody and vicious war.

His neighbours congratulated the farmer on his good fortune.

The man just said, "We'll see."

I love the simplicity of this story and its relevance to the challenges faced by new ventures.

Three things stand out for me:

- I need to avoid judging events that I have no control over as good or bad. This is an error. Luck is luck. No more, no less.
- I must be careful not to claim credit for good luck or dwell on bad.
- I will never know whether luck is good or bad until after the event, so to label it as such is not helpful.

Move mountains with your little finger

"Give me a place to stand on, and I will move the Earth." *Archimedes*

Or – in other words, "Give me a lever long enough and a fulcrum on which to place it, and I shall move the world."

Archimedes was Smart with a capital S.

What's a lever? A lever is a simple machine that consists of a beam pivoted at a fulcrum. Identified as one of the six basic machines by Renaissance scientists, its name is derived from the French word "lever", which means "to raise". Its primary function is to amplify an input force, thus providing a larger output force, a mechanism often referred to as "leverage". The ideal mechanical advantage of a lever is represented by the ratio of the output force to the input force.

In the business world, there are plenty of levers to use. Identifying them and using them to your advantage is an essential part of building a small business that can take on established rivals.

For example, Microsoft came to dominate the world of PC operating systems through a smart distribution deal with IBM. IBM at the time was a massive PC manufacturer, Microsoft was tiny. Microsoft's then-CEO, Bill Gates, managed to get his operating system into all IBM machines yet retained the rights to use them elsewhere. By leveraging the massive scale of IBM, MS DOS became the market-leading PC operating system of its time.

These days, a small online trader can leverage the marketplaces of eBay and Amazon to gain access to consumers. A gaming company can leverage the user base of Facebook. A software-as-a-service (SaaS) business can give away free products in app stores to acquire customers that they can up-sell into paying subscribers. A travel insurance provider can partner with an online travel agent to gain access to relevant consumers.

Thinking of the world in terms of how to leverage the strengths of others to your advantage is a very useful perspective when you have very little in the way of money or resources.

Chapter 2 - Choosing what to do next

Priorities, to-do lists and endless tasks at hand. Often you'll feel that it's never ending and there's no let-up. So how to prioritise? And what are you prioritising for? This is something I'll cover in the next few pages.

"No" matters more than "yes"

Back in the 1990s, I was Head of Operations for a niche upmarket tour operator, Simply Travel. It was a great company. We offered quality and authentic accommodation in some of the most beautiful destinations in Europe and provided the best possible service. We sold the business to Thomson Travel (later TUI) in 1999. In 2000, during the dotcom boom, I moved to an online travel startup.

I mention this because I'd like to thank Steve Rushton, our Managing Director at the time, for some sage advice.

I was busy, flat out. As I like to get things done well, I was worried that I was not completing everything I wanted to. Not enough "i"s were dotted or "t"s crossed. My to-do list was never ending. Steve said that if I had too much work, it wasn't important to finish everything, and that it was more important to finish the most important work first. He said something like "If you have enough work to fill 150% of your time, make sure you choose the most important 100%."

A few years later I was working at Expedia. I was with our Managing Director Dermot Halpin and we were talking about strategy. Dermot emphasised that it's not what you choose to do that defines your strategy, it's what you decide not to do. If you are not saying no, you don't have a strategy.

So often in life we want to say yes. Opportunities are around every corner. It's important to grasp these opportunities. If you are lucky enough to have more opportunities than time, what will define you is what you say no to - not what you say yes to.

That may sound counterintuitive, and it probably is. Be really good at saying no a lot. But when you do say yes, make it count.

Priority is a decision, not a status

At a traffic junction, traffic rules give one vehicle priority over the other. It's black and white. You either have priority or you don't. If you have priority, it's your turn to go first.

Priority, not priorities

When people talk about their priorities my brain waves a red flag.

I prefer to think of "What is *the* priority?", not "What are the priori*ties*?"

When you ask yourself, "What is my priority?" you are putting one thing to the top of your to-do list. It is literally at the top, because "prior" means "to put before".

We can only focus on one thing at a time. Thinking that you can multitask is a delusion. When you work on two things at the same time, you're not multitasking - you are in fact switch-tasking.

Switch-tasking is useful when you need to get feedback or input from another person before continuing with a task. However, switching between two tasks over a period of time to complete both will take you longer than simply doing one first, then the other.

Your decisions determine priority

Your decision to work on something first makes it your priority. Whatever is at the top of your to-do list is your decision.

A task does not have an in-built priority. The only thing that makes it a priority is your decision (or an instruction you receive - i.e. someone else's decision) to make it so.

"This is a high priority task" is a term you hear in offices around the world. It's an obscure statement. All it tells you is that it's one of many important things. "My priority is to do X" is better. It commits you more to the outcome and forces a decision on what is important at that moment in time.

You cannot have two priorities. One is always more important than the other. But I hear you say, "What if they are equally important?" Think about it. Are two things ever equally important? Perhaps. But you can still only start one first. That one is your priority.

(To be clear, I do still consider it useful to think about what the most important things are and have that as a shortlist. I simply want to reserve the word "priority" for whatever is at the top of that shortlist. If I can't progress the priority and it's blocked, I can switch to task number two until the priority task is unblocked.)

To prioritise is to triage

An emergency room (ER in the US, A&E in the UK) at a hospital has to deal with the continual challenge of new urgent and important cases being brought to them. Yet there are only so many doctors and response teams.

A critical function of an effective ER is triage. To decide the order in which a large number of patients or casualties should be attended to, triage nurses first assess the degree of urgency for treating their wounds or illnesses. At any given moment, one case takes priority over all the others. It comes first.

To be prior is to come before - to be first.

Being more efficient doesn't always generate more success

What are you optimising for - and why? This question lies at the heart of organisational design.

It's a question that often goes unasked. Many people joining a startup from more mature organisations are inclined to optimise for efficiency. Once you have a business model that works, optimising for efficiency can make sense. It can be overdone too - think of all those hours you've wasted waiting in phone queuing systems. They might be efficient for the large company, but they are not giving a great experience to the consumer.

There are always different ways to optimise.

You could optimise for:

- learning
- reputation
- growth
- quality
- speed
- cost

Which one to choose? At HouseTrip I had a triple challenge.

First, our operations team had to keep up with growth. We were growing at more than 10% per month. That meant, unless we changed the way we worked, we needed 10% more people, every month. In fact, our Lisbon customer service team grew from two to 90 people in 12 months.

The second challenge was to improve service quality. We started measuring our customer satisfaction with the service received and then systematically found ways to improve it.

Third, we had to gradually reduce the cost of servicing a booking. That meant removing unnecessary enquiries by improving the core product as well as providing better self-help tools. It also meant helping the team to be more efficient with better tools including a library of pre-written responses.

One thing I learnt fast was that above all else we should optimise for quality.

The way to do that was to use both qualitative and quantitative data and -

most importantly - organise the team around the customer. At one point we made the mistake of creating too many specialist teams, each focussing on one particular task, such as handling complaints, payment queries or host relations. This helped us create expertise, but with an unfortunate side-effect - it slowed things down, because several people were involved in solving each case.

In contrast, we found that the single most important driver of customer satisfaction was speed of response. Therefore, we needed team members who could deal with as much of an issue on their own - and who had the authority to make refund decisions (up to a point). This increased the speed of responses and the quality of customer experience.

We optimised for quality by organising ourselves around the customer experience.

We don't always ask ourselves what we are optimising for. In modern business it's often around efficiency. I'd argue that it's always worth stepping back to ask what matters most at the time and agree out loud that this is what you are optimising for. Then, and only then, define the problems and search for solutions.

Plants need water to grow - so do businesses

Plants need sunlight. They also need water, some more than others. They need liquidity. Water is life.

Businesses need liquidity too. We often think of liquidity in terms of cash flow - a company's ability to convert assets to cash.

There's another way of thinking of liquidity. Instead of cash flow, think of supply and demand. How can a company best use its supply to create demand? Or vice versa, how can you use your demand to generate new supply?

Good liquidity is achieved when there is enough supply to attract demand and there is enough demand to attract supply. It's the critical mass that provides the momentum to get the business moving.

I've spent the best part of my career operating, growing or investing in online marketplaces. In these businesses, liquidity is key. But not all liquidity has the same value. Let me explain.

Chicken and egg

One of the challenges in growing any marketplace is getting it up and running in the first place.

Buyers won't visit a marketplace if there is nothing to buy. Sellers won't sell at a marketplace unless there are buyers.

As with the chicken and the egg, which comes first?

At any moment in time, most marketplaces need to invest in one side of the business to also stimulate the other. For example, they may need to invest in onboarding more sellers to then attract more buyers - or vice versa. The side that requires investment may change over time.

One thing is certain: a large consumer base is a good reason for sellers to want to use the service. But this doesn't always work in reverse; just because you have a large number of products on the shelves doesn't mean people will come.

Start simple - one channel, one segment, one product

Successful marketplaces don't launch everywhere to everyone at once. There's usually a starting point with a simple supply base and a narrow consumer base. Only once these small-scale operations have proven the business model should the marketplace expand to a wider supply base with a larger target audience.

As I mentioned earlier, I always like to think of it this way. Find one customer segment willing to buy one product type through one channel. Do this well. Then expand from there.

In 1983 - 40 years ago - Gerry Pack founded Holiday Extras (where I now work) by selling one product (airport hotels) to one segment (holidaymakers booking via travel agents in the UK) through one channel (the telephone). This was a win-win-win situation. It was a win for travel agents, which had previously had to contact airport hotels one by one to find availability but now found it easy to make bookings. It was a win for hoteliers, who generated lots of business from the travel trade. And it was a win for Holiday Extras, which earned commission from hotels.

Later, Holiday Extras expanded with additional product lines (airport parking, travel insurance, etc.), additional channels (online booking) and additional customer segments (business travel, the German market).

Think of Amazon. It started with just one product category (books), in one market (the US). Amazon focussed on building liquidity with books and US consumers, built an early customer base and supply base, built an operating model and - later - added additional products such as CDs.

Over the years Amazon has increased liquidity by adding new product categories and opening in new markets, and has gone on to allow other retailers to sell via its platform. It didn't do all of this on day one.

Let's look at an example of how another startup - Snaptrip - tackled the liquidity challenge. Snaptrip is a travel startup in which we invested at Forward Partners. Snaptrip brings together last-minute holiday cottage deals into a single platform, allowing holidaymakers to find a bargain by comparing available options quickly.

In getting started, it was important for Snaptrip to find a way to validate its consumer proposition quickly without having to build a large supply base (which would have increased the time to launch). The first step of building liquidity was to create a modest pond - rather than a large ocean - of suppliers. It signed up one accommodation agency in the Lake District (a popular destination for UK holidaymakers) and then used Google AdWords (now Google Ads) to serve adverts based on keywords used by bookers who were looking for accommodation in the region.

From this pond, Snaptrip started fishing. It managed to attract consumers, create bookings for its first supplier and validate its proposition (last-minute rentals at great discounts). This phase provided deep insights into consumer buying preferences and supplier needs. The next step was to take this learning and tweak the product and service. Snaptrip then expanded its supply, region by region, in order to achieve national coverage. Note that it didn't go for national coverage on day one.

Whenever I work with or advise early-stage marketplace businesses, I always ask what kind of liquidity they need to grow. There are different types of liquidity and achieving liquidity at one level can help you power up to the next.

Do you grow your supply on a category-by-category basis (like Amazon) or on a location-by-location basis (like Snaptrip)? Do you grow your demand by consumer segment, neighbourhood, language or interest?

Getting this growth model right is an important consideration and can be the difference between success and failure.

Getting a trickle of liquidity across a wide area isn't as useful as getting a torrent of liquidity in a focussed area. This is because once liquidity starts to build, it becomes self-sustaining, delivers economies of scale and provides an enduring competitive advantage.

If a marketplace can be broken down into separate units of liquidity, each unit can be treated as a startup in its own right. Some units will be in a set-up phase, some will be in an investment phase and others will be profitable. This provides a roadmap for product development, marketing and commercial focus that would otherwise be lacking with a do-everything-at-once approach.

Here are some liquidity factors to consider:

Supply

- Nationwide versus city versus neighbourhood
- Cross category versus one category
- Direct versus indirect suppliers

Demand

- Nationwide versus city versus neighbourhood
- Business to business versus business to consumer
- Interest groups
- Language

I will illustrate the point with a number of examples.

Bookatable - Cities
Bookatable was a leading restaurant-booking website and app. I was COO

there during the early growth phase. Restaurant bookings are generally focussed on city centres and so we concentrated on building a critical mass of restaurants city by city, providing a range of choice and availability to consumers. A lot of search traffic was destination led, so we were able to capture demand showing intent to book a table in London, Hamburg and Stockholm, etc. Liquidity was achieved when we became an essential source of bookings for the restaurants in these cities.

HouseTrip - Corridors

When I was at HouseTrip, a holiday rentals marketplace, we identified that supply and demand flowed through corridors between origins and destinations. Origins are countries where customers live (such as the UK, France or Germany), and destinations are resorts or cities that they visit (such as Mallorca, Paris or the Amalfi Coast). The UK to Mallorca is one corridor, as is Germany to Mallorca. As such, we built up supply on a destination-by-destination basis and then worked on building demand from one origin to that destination, then another origin and then another origin.

Hassle.com - Neighbourhoods

Hassle.com (later called Helping) offered domestic cleaning services. Customers searched on Hassle.com for cleaners near them. Hassle.com took their booking details and sent them to local cleaners who competed for the work. For Hassle.com to succeed, it needed enough cleaners in each neighbourhood to service the demand in that neighbourhood. This is because cleaners tend to work a few hours at a time and need to have a number of clients without too much travel time between them. It makes sense in this kind of marketplace to build liquidity neighbourhood by neighbourhood, city by city.

Unlocking a growth engine

Supply can be a growth lever. Each time a new product category, destination or neighbourhood is added, it gives more choice to the consumer and can increase conversions. (That is, provided you can attract consumers.) More conversions equal better marketing efficiency, allowing more money to be invested in customer acquisition at the top of the funnel.

However, adding a new supply category requires a set-up phase and, for a period of time, investment. Each marketplace business needs to understand how many new supply segments it can realistically onboard at once and what the return on investment looks like for each segment.

Getting this right can unlock a virtuous growth engine. Each new supply segment adds to the liquidity of the overall offering.

Gaining a good understanding of what type of liquidity is needed is the first step towards building a growth strategy for a marketplace. But this is also true for many different types of business, from B2C retail to B2B software.

Invest in organisational debt and have a plan to pay it back

In the early days of a business, it's just not possible to create an entire company and all the streamlined processes and systems you'd like from day one. These things take time, money and focus, which are in scarce supply at the outset. Sometimes you need to hack temporary solutions. For example, until you've built your back office system, you might have people doing manual work to make it all happen behind the scenes. Similarly, you might outsource a function to a third party until you're big enough to do it in house.

These temporary hacks represent a kind of "organisational debt". And until you've replaced them with more comprehensive solutions, systems or processes, the price you'll pay could include complexity, delays in gathering information or bigger salary overheads than needed to complete a task.

(Organisational debt is a concept similar to technical debt. Technical debt refers to situations when suboptimal code is produced by software engineers to get a feature or product out the door quickly. There's often a good reason to do this, such as winning a new client or testing a new concept cheaply, but it does mean that at some point someone is going to need to refactor the code and build the system properly, and until they do so the code base is more difficult to maintain. The interest that you pay on this debt is the increasing complexity of the code base. This makes new developments more difficult to write, test or ship, means there are more bugs to fix and has a knock-on effect on the morale of the development team.)

Taking on organisational debt makes sense if you are still developing and testing the business model.

Startups are organisations in search of a viable and repeatable business model. Investing in processes and systems only makes sense once there are customers to serve and revenues being generated.

Larger companies with innovation projects are in some ways also like startups - they are searching for viable and repeatable new revenue streams.

In both cases, there's a right time to take out debt and there's a right time to pay it back.

Scaling a business with a lot of organisational debt is risky. An organisation that works at 100 transactions a day could self-destruct at 1,000 transactions a day if there are lots of manual processes. In the same way that taking on more financial debt than you can handle can put you at risk of bankruptcy, organisational debt can cripple an organisation trying to scale.

In what order should you pay back the debt?

Here's how I prioritise which type of organisational debt to repay first:

1. First, I consider which processes and systems are closest to the customer and optimise them. Above all else, the business needs customers and it needs great customer experience. If it affects the customer experience, fix that first.
2. Next, I focus on fixing the unit economics of the business. This allows the business to start generating a better contribution from each transaction and gives a good base from which to scale.
3. Later, I optimise the back office and overheads. Examples might be customer service systems, finance systems or procurement.

If a business was scaling and addressing point 3 before points 1 or 2, it would cause me concern. If 1 and 2 are getting good attention, it builds a good base from which to optimise point 3.

Of course, this model involves huge generalisation but it's the best way I've found to express why it's OK to maintain some organisational debt as you grow.

It's OK to have the right kind of debt

As a startup COO (Chief Operating Officer) I often had colleagues proposing ideas or projects that improved the efficiencies of the business. If these were in category 3 and we hadn't yet fixed 1 or 2, I would say that it was better to hold off on these projects and suffer the ongoing organisational headaches until we'd built a business worth optimising.

Startups often have a bumpy ride after raising growth funding, as some parts of the business mature before the rest have caught up. It can feel very difficult for the people involved, and the challenge for the management team is to help people understand that it's a conscious decision to hold off on improving some parts of the business because it makes sense to be in debt in that area at that time.

I think it's about recognising and sharing with the team that "Yes, we can and should do better (in the area that is chaotic). We will fix it, but now is not the right time." It's not an easy thing to communicate and requires sharing with the team the big picture about what areas are improving and why they are important pieces of the jigsaw to solve first.

As always, it's about prioritising and not taking on more debt than you can handle.

Quality is something you need to lock in

A process is a simple but important tool in the growth manager's toolkit.

Processes lock in quality. As the company spins forward to growth, processes ensure that high-quality activity is repeatable.

Processes are built upon principles

The more clearly you state your principles and the more they are understood by the team, the less you will need overly detailed instructions in your processes and the more autonomous the team will be.

Examples of principles:

- We will always attempt to acknowledge a customer complaint within 24 hours of receipt.
- We will match any competitor price for the same goods if we receive notice within two weeks of purchase.
- We will/will not cover shipping costs for returns.

- We will ensure all new starters have a desk, computer and email account set up prior to their start date.

Processes are built upon principles into a set of repeatable instructions or methods that explain how individuals, teams and systems act out the principles. A process describes step by step what is required in a particular scenario. It usually also explains who is responsible at each stage.

Examples of processes:

- How to deal with a cancellation
- How we recruit people
- How we handle complaints
- What we do when someone leaves the company

Describing a process without explaining the principles that underpin it creates the risk that people following the instructions won't appreciate the context in which they are working. Blindly following instructions means that if those instructions are missing a small point of detail, or if the circumstances are so unusual that the instructions are incomplete, a team member may not know how to act. However, if team members can understand the principles upon which the instructions are based, they are more able to act in the interests of the company and of the customer.

Just as a machine might allow continuous motion in only one direction while preventing motion in the opposite direction by means of a gear and pawl mounted on a base (known as a ratchet system), creating process in a scaling business can ensure quality and consistency to avoid slipping back into more inconsistent and chaotic outcomes.

I find processes are best co-created with the people who already do the work, not the people managing the work, ideally through a collaborative approach.

Ideally, every process should also be measured with KPIs so people know how well the process is working and, most importantly, can review and change it regularly. If a process never changes, it will never improve, so always revisit and improve processes where you can.

However, you can have too much process. You can over-engineer and over-optimise, which can strangle growth and agility. Equally, you can have too little. You might have processes that worked well for you last year but which no longer work this year, because you've grown. The balance I'd recommend is to have processes, "but only just enough."

Complex is not always complicated

Don't "complex" and "complicated" mean the same thing?

Not necessarily. There's a subtle, but very interesting, difference between the two.

A complicated system has many connected and related parts and importantly, it is difficult to understand.

A complex system however also has many interacting parts, but it has simple individual rules that deliver versatile emergent properties.

An example of a complex system is a flock of birds. Two simple rules might control the overall system: alignment of flight direction in comparison to the nearest bird and distance between neighbouring birds. These two variables are all that's needed to understand and change the system.

Complicated systems, such as space rockets, have many more variables. The more complicated you make a machine, the more likely it will fail. The same is true of business processes.

One of my favourite sayings is "Complicated problems do not need complicated solutions."

If you can identify the simple drivers that influence the emergent behaviour, you can focus on these simple changes.

Complicated problems are often best solved with simple solutions.

Uncertainty is not risk

A short note on the difference between the two.

> "The practical difference between the two categories, risk and uncertainty, is that in the former the distribution of the outcome in a group of instances is known (either through calculation a priori or from statistics of past experience), while in the case of uncertainty this is not true, the reason being in general that it is impossible to form a group of instances, because the situation dealt with is in a high degree unique." *Frank Knight, Risk, Uncertainty and Profit (1921)*

Risk of falling off your bike = known potential outcomes.

Uncertainty of the future of European Union government = unknown potential outcomes.

Risks are therefore the known unknowns.

Uncertainties are the unknown unknowns.

Companies operate in a world of uncertainty, and they need to identify risks to their business model, address these risks and do what they can to reduce uncertainty.

Scaling is not growth

Some startups become scale-ups. Scale-ups? What is scaling? In today's language it usually means investing for growth.

By investing for growth, the company gets to scale, i.e. becomes larger. This scale-up phase typically is funded with growth capital, often starting with Series A venture capital.

Good scaling

Simply put, scaling up should only happen once there is a viable and repeatable business model.

The business may not yet be profitable but it has figured out how to repeatedly acquire customers at a price that makes sense. It knows who its core customers are and where to reach them, and has a product that meets their needs.

Not only that, but it won't just be a product that meets their needs, it will be a great product. To define "great", I like to refer to Sean Ellis (co-author of *Hacking Growth*, known best for coining the phrase "growth hacking") and his must-have product question.

He asks customers, "How would you feel if you could no longer use [product]?"

The answer choices are:

- Very disappointed
- Somewhat disappointed
- Not disappointed (it isn't really that useful)
- N/A - I no longer use [product].

In his research he found that if more than 40% of respondents answer "Very disappointed", you probably have a must-have product.

A must-have product means two things:

- Customers will be loyal, so retention will be high.
- Customers will be easier (and cheaper) to acquire.

However, even with a great product, the startup needs to also have a clear path to profitability.

Business-model fit, a must-have product and a clear path to profitability are good checks for whether a startup is ready to scale.

I also like to think of scaling in terms of "economies of scale".

Here's a simple example. You have £100,000 in revenue. You have five people. You have two web servers.

What happens when you double the revenue? Do you double the team and double the number of servers? If you do, you are not scaling. You are just growing.

Scaling would mean that you doubled the revenue, but the team size and web servers did not need to double. Maybe the team expanded to six people and the number of web servers stayed the same. Now you're starting to scale.

Bad scaling

A startup raises seed money and gets going. Unless it becomes very profitable very quickly, it's likely that more funding will be needed.

This can be a problem if the cash runs out before the conditions for scaling have been met.

Some startups launch larger onward funding rounds, despite the fact that they are not actually ready to scale. They pitch to investors, the investors buy the story, and they raise the money.

The money is in the bank and then there's pressure to deliver on the (flawed) business plan presented to investors. More money is spent on marketing and more salespeople are hired. But because the basic unit economics are not in place, the monthly cash burn just goes through the roof.

The result? Crash and burn.

To scale, do things that don't scale

Something scalable is something that can be done in a repeated, predictable way. It's efficient. It could be automated or done in bulk.

It could be how you deliver training to new starters or how you publish your weekly reports. It could be how you integrate a new supplier or how you add a new market.

Sometimes scaling is achieved through coding, sometimes through process.

I have often found that it's important to do things manually at first before trying to create efficiency. When you do something manually, you might not be at all efficient but what you are doing is learning. You are learning what problems need to be solved, you understand how frequently these problems need to be solved and you can try new ways of solving this problem. If you need to change a solution you can do it quickly.

At the beginning, it's important to optimise for learning, not for efficiency. Later, when the problem and solution are fully understood and there is predictability in how to solve the problem, you can automate or focus on productivity.

Paradoxically, even when you could scale the process, sometimes it pays not to.

"David, we have this process that we are doing which takes 12 hours every week. If we automated it, we could do it in 15 minutes!"

I ask how long it would take to code a solution.

"It'd take about a week to deliver this project."

Then I ask how much it would cost to solve the problem with people, and how much it would cost to write the code. And I realise that the costs are about the same. Furthermore, there is an opportunity cost. My software developer could be working on something that creates extra revenue with that time. I would rather have them do that. And then if we did automate the solution, if the solution changed we would have to rewrite it. Sometimes it's actually better just to keep doing things in the "inefficient" way.

At a leadership level too, sometimes it pays to do the work that someone below your pay grade would do - at least while you get the project started. If you are the one talking to customers, understanding the problem and developing the solution, it will help you understand what's needed to scale it. I believe a strong leader needs to know when to get their hands dirty (when going after new value) and when to step back and focus on the process rather than the work (when the value is established).

You then are in a better position to scale, because you are scaling something that has known value, that is understood and that is predictable. But you only know that because you did things that didn't scale.

Chapter 3 - Setting objectives and measuring progress

If you've managed to prioritise your work, hopefully you are making progress towards your goals. Are you? It's very easy to become despondent if all you focus on is what's next on your list. Standing back to measure progress gives you a sense of perspective and, importantly, tells you if your effort is on track.

Knowing why can be more important than knowing how

Between the First World War and the Second World War one of the world's most formidable fighting forces developed. It was an army with 4,000 senior commanders. It was the German *Wehrmacht*.

If I were a soldier in the British or Russian Army at that time and we were approaching a riverside town, my commanding officer might tell me to attack a specific outpost or take the square. Once I had completed that task I would radio in for new orders.

If I were a soldier in the German army at the time, the officer might tell me that the objective was to quickly secure the bridge to the other side of the river. I might need to take the town square to do that. If things didn't go to plan, I could think on my feet and figure out my next move, knowing the intent of the commanding officer without knowing his precise instructions and without asking for permission to change direction.

This is the concept of mission-driven tactics, also known as *Auftragstaktik*.

Auftragstaktik encourages commanders to exhibit initiative, flexibility and improvisation while in command. It was developed by the Prussians in the 19th century, after their defeat at the hands of Napoleon Bonaparte, and took a century to mature.

With knowledge of the mission (the why), the unit leaders had more freedom to pursue the how and react in real time.

Here's the doctrine described by the German army.

Auftragstaktik is the pre-eminent command and control principle in the Army. It is based on mutual trust and requires each soldier's unwavering commitment to perform his duty. The military leader informs what his intention is, sets clear achievable objectives, and provides the required forces and resources. He will only order details regarding execution if measures which serve the same objective have to be harmonised, if political or military constraints require it. He gives latitude to subordinate leaders in the execution of their mission.

This method, if employed well, is extremely effective in times of uncertainty. It's counterintuitive to the top-down command and control hierarchies that are typical of 20th century industrialised western economies.

It seems to me that business in the modern age is fraught with uncertainty and, while we may not be an army fighting a war, the ability to adapt to change quickly will be the make or break of modern companies.

Objectives and Key Results (OKRs)

The well-known concept of objectives and key results (OKRs) has been written about extensively elsewhere. I mention OKRs because, if done well, they provide a strong direction and definition of success for the team and are the equivalent of military mission-driven tactics.

The "objective" is the change we are trying to make. The "key results" are what we will deliver if we succeed.

When writing objectives, I find it always helps to start the statement with a verb.

For example:

- Prove that customers aged 18-25 are willing to buy our product.
- Expand our customer base in London.
- Improve the efficiency of our shipping operation.

And when writing key results, describe a measurable result.

For example:

- Conversion for 18-25-year-old buyers reaches 90%+ of other age groups.
- 1,000 new London household customers are acquired by the end of the quarter.
- Shipping costs decrease from 3% of revenue to 2% of revenue.

None of these objectives or key results describe the how. They leave it open. This means you can try one tactic to achieve the mission and, if it doesn't work (as determined by the key results), then you can try another. It really helps communicate the mission and what success looks like. OKRs give teams more freedom to adapt and make decisions on how best to reach their objective without asking for permission.

A word of warning. I have used OKRs in many different situations and in different companies. I have not found an OKR methodology that works every time in every company. I've usually had to adapt it to make it work for the situation. Sometimes OKRs work well as group goals (e.g. at a team and/or company level) - but not always. Sometimes they can also work at an individual level - but not always.

That's why I would steer away from OKR software solutions as a first step. I'd work with your team to develop a system that works for you. Later, once you've been through several cycles, you'll know how you and your team use them best and then you can evaluate software (or not) based on your needs.

There's a K in KPI

Successful growth leaders know their metrics. In conversation they will recall numbers with clarity and be able to explain their context. But this doesn't just happen. To know what's going on, they measure, report and analyse.

The trouble is there's so much you can measure. It's easy to drown in data. I've seen KPI dashboards that have so much data it takes half an hour to go through them.

There's a K in KPI. K is for "key". *Key* Performance Indicators. Some metrics matter more than others.

How do you know you're focussing on the right KPIs?

Key metrics are those metrics which, if trending well, suggest the whole business is moving in the right direction. And because "key" means "of crucial importance", you'll be working with just a few numbers - not 20 or even 10.

Focus on the outcomes. In my experience, before deciding which numbers matter most, the first question you need to ask is, "What outcome am I looking for?"

Example outcomes are:

- I can identify potential customers.
- I can convert prospects to customers.
- Customers have a great experience.

- I have a profitable marketing channel.
- Our customers return and buy again.
- Our people are happy.

Once you start framing the business challenge in this kind of language, you will have a clearer idea of what you need to measure.

Outcomes change as the business evolves

For startups, there are a number of outcomes to achieve before the business becomes viable. There's a logical order in which each of these outcomes is best achieved before moving on to the next.

For example, it makes sense to have a product that people love before spending a lot of money on marketing it.

Net promoter score (NPS) is a metric that can be used as a good measure of customer love. (NPS asks customers "On a scale from 0 to 10, how likely are you to recommend this product/company to a friend or colleague?" The score is calculated by subtracting the percentage of customers who answer the question with a rating of 6 or lower (detractors) from the percentage of customers who answer with a 9 or 10 (promoters). The resulting score is on a scale from -100 to +100.)

However, once the product is loved, the emphasis might shift to improving the conversion rate of prospects to buyers (while maintaining or improving NPS). After that, the emphasis might swing to optimising the cost of customer acquisition (again while maintaining or improving NPS).

As such, the metrics that matter most will change until the business model settles. Once the company is in growth mode the outcomes needed will stabilise.

Revenue is an end result, not a KPI

This is important to understand. The amount of money you are making (or not) is the end result of your business activity. Focussing on revenue will not increase revenue. Focussing on the things that drive revenue will increase revenue. Sure, you need to track your revenues and reference them, but that doesn't always make revenue a KPI.

Things that might drive revenue include the net promoter score, repeat user rate, conversion rate, cost of customer acquisition and referral rate.

In fact, there's an argument that you should pick one metric above all others as the one to optimise for. Known in lean analytics as "the one metric that matters", this number changes as the business develops.

Metrics have a hierarchy

Examining the relationships between the different metrics in your business is a useful exercise. You can draw these out as a tree.

As an example, let's use conversion rate and net margin:

You have 1,000 visits.

- You have 10 sales (1% convert).
- You make £1,000 in sales (each transaction is worth on average £100).
- You make £200 in net margin (you have a 20% margin).

What things can increase net margin?

- Total visits can increase transactions (all else being equal).
- Conversion rate can increase transactions (all else being equal).
- Average sales value can increase total sales (all else being equal).

- Margin % can increase net margin (all else being equal).

Map out your metrics on a whiteboard. Understand what factors influence others. This will help you to understand which metrics matter.

What time frame?

Should you report on your numbers on a daily, weekly or monthly basis? All of the above.

There are two principles to guide you:

1. Think about what you need to measure daily, weekly and monthly, based on how meaningful the data is across those time frames. For some metrics, you need a decent number of events in order to get a meaningful number. For example, if you measured conversion rate on a daily basis yet only had a handful of visitors, the results would vary so wildly that they would be meaningless. You'd need a week of data to make sense of it.
2. Think about how important it is that you react to changes in the observed numbers. If by observing something on a daily basis you can make a change that day that improves the performance the following day, then daily monitoring makes sense. Otherwise, some metrics might be better observed on a weekly basis.

KPIs are only useful if they are shared

Consider how and when you share the data.

There are different ways that you can surface metrics for discussion and review, such as:

- Daily stand-up

- Daily email
- Whiteboard
- Monitor screen
- Weekly team meeting
- Weekly email
- Monthly management reporting pack
- Board meetings

Aim to socialise the data in a way that helps the team make decisions.

While real-time dashboards and tools are useful, sometimes you need to consolidate the data into a single view.

As a COO, I liked using a Google Sheet to gather and record weekly numbers. We had a distributed team and specific team members were responsible for gathering and entering the data into the sheet. We had a Monday afternoon call each week to look at the numbers together and decide what actions we needed to take. The call created an incentive for everyone to complete their data collection on time.

I also liked having a historical view that was available on one sheet. I didn't need to go to different tools to look at the data - it was all in one place.

Data in, data out

Finally, it's worth noting that the data you get out is only as good as the data you put in.

Start with your outcomes and then ask yourself what tools, systems or processes you need to gather data to measure those outcomes. Don't start with the tools and report what they give you. Just because tools can measure certain metrics doesn't mean that those metrics are meaningful for measuring your business by.

Spend time testing your tools and making sure that the data is solid before you rely on it.

A word of warning. As Dan Ariely (author of *Predictably Irrational*) pointed out in his Harvard Business Review column "You Are What You Measure" in 2010:

> "Human beings adjust behavior based on the metrics they're held against. Anything you measure will impel a person to optimize his score on that metric. What you measure is what you'll get. Period."

Choosing the wrong metrics to focus on can drastically alter your behaviour and that of your team.

That's why it's so important to think carefully about what you are measuring and why. It can make all the difference. Choose the key things that really do matter given the stage in your company development.

KPIs don't mean anything without context

KPIs on their own have very little meaning. Context gives meaning.

At a board meeting I attended, when we came to review the main numbers (revenues, sales, marketing expenses etc.) all I really wanted to know was why. On this occasion we were not provided with any commentary in the board pack, just the numbers.

Numbers by themselves have limited meaning. Do we know why we did better than expected on sales? (If so, let's design to do more of that.)

Do we know why the marketing efficiency decreased? (Were others bidding higher than usual, was there a conversion issue, etc.? Let's figure this out to avoid repeating.)

Do we know why the support load increased? (Was something broken on the site, do we have a supplier issue, was it because we did more bookings? Therefore, is an increase in support issues a problem or not?)

Numbers are headlines. You need a story to make sense of a headline.

Other numbers can provide part of the story. For example, when looking at marketing efficiency, or return on investment (ROI), you would also look at click-through rate, cost per click, conversion rate, and so on. These numbers provide context - to a certain point - if you know what you're looking at.

Think of KPIs like a pyramid. At the top is the most important number. Under that are the most important numbers that affect the most important number. Under each of these are the numbers that in turn most influence the secondary numbers.

Despite having well-structured numbers, we still need commentary (in words) to get the full picture.

This type of information is invaluable and provides meaning. For example:

- Positive - our promotion with partner A exceeded all expectations and improved sales by X% (we had forecast Y%).
- Negative - the site had a partial outage for 18 hours on dd/mm due to an unforeseen problem with our content delivery network. This reduced conversion by X% for the week. We have taken precautions to avoid this scenario in future.

Ultimately, a leader or anyone working on growth initiatives needs to have a clear view of the business and demonstrate a good understanding of any influences on performance.

This needs words *and* numbers, not just numbers.

If you can't measure customer behaviour, understand it instead

On day one of a new business initiative there may be very little customer data. The founders or leaders will have an understanding of a problem that exists, and they will have an idea of how they might solve that problem.

In comparison, in a later-stage business in a high-growth phase, there can be stacks of useful data.

There is a transition that happens from the early days of a company/project to its later growth stages in terms of the types of customer data gathered and used.

Useful customer data at the beginning is mainly qualitative. At the later stage the emphasis turns to quantitative.

This is a simplistic model and reality will differ on a case-by-case basis. At no point would I advise any company to rely purely on qualitative or quantitative data sources.

Qualitative data is the useful data gathered from unstructured sources such as customer interviews. Sentiments, intentions, motives and behaviours can be understood (to a certain degree.)

Quantitative data, on the other hand, is the useful data gathered from structured sources such as clicks, conversion rate, basket size, repeat visit rate, net promoter score and cost per conversion, etc.

It's important to uncover as much useful customer data as possible at each step of the journey. In the early days the team can conduct customer interviews. Landing page experiments can be conducted to capture customer contact details. You can then ask these customers questions and start to really understand their needs.

Tracking should be baked in from the outset so activity data can be gathered. This quantitative data becomes more reliable as more visits and transactions take place.

Once transactions become more frequent and predictable, the team can set up optimisation tests such as split tests.

The questions that are asked change along the way. We shift our emphasis from who, why and what towards when, how often and how much. For example, we start with questions like "How do we know our customers have a problem?" and "Are our customers willing to pay for solving that problem?" Later on, we ask different questions, such as "Are we improving conversion?" and "What is the cost of customer acquisition?"

To answer these questions, sometimes you need conversations and sometimes you need tracking tools and numbers.

Both are important.

Every customer service issue is a failure of your product

A few years ago, I was chatting with Matt Witt (a non-exec Director and operations consultant) about the challenges that online companies have with building out their customer service operations.

Witt had been COO at Active Hotels, a phenomenally successful hotel booking website that was acquired by Booking.com. At the time, I was COO at HouseTrip, one of Europe's fast-growing startups.

Matt explained that he viewed any customer service issue as a failure of the product. If a customer needed to call up or email to resolve an issue, that was an opportunity to improve the product. If customers repeatedly complain about the same things, your operations are not scaling. As the old adage goes, you can only make the same mistake once - the second time it's a choice. While I had intuitively understood this to be true, Matt's explicit statement stuck in my mind.

I learnt that it's important to measure and categorise the issues that are received. For example:

- How many issues (daily, weekly)?
- From where in the product do they originate?
- What is the time spent per type of issue?
- What type of customers have the issue?
- Were the issues easily resolved?
- What was the cost of each issue type?
- What is the customer satisfaction rate for customers that contact you (by issue type)?

With this kind of data you can start to build prevention and improvement strategies.

For example, you can start to improve the self-help areas of your customer experience, on the phone or via the web. More importantly, you can give structured feedback to the product team about the customer experience and work together on improvements that will prevent the issues from recurring.

As mentioned previously, at HouseTrip we had a three-way challenge concerning customer service:

1. Growing the customer service function fast (bookings were growing in double-digit % every month)
2. Constantly increasing the customer satisfaction rates (quality)
3. Improving efficiency of the customer service function (cost of service as a % of net revenue).

Whilst we did manage all three over time, it was important to understand the relative priority of each. Our priority was excellent customer satisfaction. We then had to cope with growth. Efficiency improvements did happen but they came later.

My advice to startups that are starting their customer service operations is to have a relentless emphasis on quality of service first and foremost, making sure to constantly improve the product to avoid issues happening in the first place.

Part 2 - question prompts

Before we move on to Part 3, here are some questions you can ask yourself to find your own growth opportunities.

> If your path is unclear, can you at least work out the next step you might take, and take it?

> Are you focussed on building a product that customers love before spending a lot on marketing?

> What could you improve further with your product, service, processes, communications or culture? What have you not looked at recently that might deserve a refresh?

> Do you regard events as good or bad (when in reality they might be neither in the long term)?

> How might you leverage a small effort to gain a strong advantage? Who could you partner with to achieve your business goals?

> Do you say yes when perhaps you should say no more?

> Do you select a clear priority to work on or do you fall into the trap of thinking you can handle multiple priorities?

> Are you clear on what you are optimising for?

> What kind of liquidity do you need with your supply and demand to fuel growth?

> Are you carrying enough or too much organisational debt?

> Are you building standardised processes to ensure that you lock in quality?

> Can you solve complicated problems with a simple solution?

> Are you keeping a risk register, and are you clear on the difference between risk and uncertainty?

> Are you making your business more efficient as it increases in size?

> Can you do the detailed work needed to get things started yet also delegate it once it's up and working?

> Do you take time to explain the "why" every time you brief your team?

>Are you clear on what are your most important measures of success, and are these tracked and communicated on a regular basis?

> When you share your KPIs, are you providing your audience with the right context to understand the implications?

> Are you gathering qualitative data on your customer experience? Is this feeding back into the development of your product/service?

> What problems would you fix to reduce the incoming contact your service team receive?

4

Part 3: Delivering growth - Building and leading teams

Chapter 1 - Hiring

To deliver on your business growth opportunity, you'll need a team. Putting together and onboarding your team is a key part of a leader's job in a growth business. In one company I probably spent one third of my time hiring. It was probably the most important third of my work.

The candidate is the job description

The job description is what the hiring manager thinks they want.

The candidate sees it and says, "I could do that."

The candidate applies and manages to get an interview. The interview goes well.

The hiring manager says, "I want to hire this person (even though they're not quite an exact match for the job description)."

The offer is made and, soon after, the candidate starts.

The job description is forgotten.

The role becomes what the candidate wants it to be and is capable of - reality rarely matches a hiring manager's initial job description.

In any role, the candidate will shape the job role as much as the job role shapes the candidate. We are all strangely unique individuals and what we bring to work every day (our skills, our interest, our knowledge, our biases, our energy, our network, our values and our motivations) turns a job description into reality. There will be things in the original job description that we don't do. There will be other things we can do and want to do which are not in the job description.

This is especially the case for startups. This is because as much as you try and write a job description that matches what you think you need in your team now, that will change within six months in a startup - things move very fast.

Instead of asking, "Will this candidate meet my job description?", try instead asking, "If this candidate could create their ideal job, what would it be?"

If that ideal job of theirs sounds like the kind of challenge you could offer, now and into the future, you might just have found a great match. A job description therefore should be thought of as an advert to attract great people. It's marketing.

Remember though that who you end up hiring will determine what actually gets done.

You are the one stopping yourself from filling the role, not the candidate

In a candidate's market, speed matters.

"I had a great developer, a fantastic candidate," said the tech recruiter of a startup I was chatting with.

"He had another offer. He was keen on the other company and so I had to move fast. I spoke with my CEO to get an interview booked in, but he was busy and couldn't offer up a slot in his calendar until the next week," he continued.

He said that the CEO quipped: "If he likes us, he'll wait. If he can't wait a week, he's not right for us."

The recruiter explained what happened next.

"I lost the candidate; he took the other job. In tech recruitment, speed matters. You need to be fast. Speed is your weapon and can be the one thing that makes the difference."

It's a simple lesson. If you really want the best candidate, they will be in demand. If you move fast, you increase your odds of success.

That means finding time, re-scheduling other meetings or sacrificing other projects to prioritise hiring. Great recruiters know this, but they need their decision makers to think this way too.

Your weaknesses are your strengths

We've all been there.

In a job interview someone asks, "Tell me about your strengths."

It's easy for most of us to answer something on this one.

Then, "Tell me about your weaknesses." Hmmm, tricky. Just how honest do you get? I bet most people are less than honest.

If you say, "I don't have any", that's a weakness in itself. You're not self-aware.

As an interviewer, the purpose of these questions is to assess self-awareness. Self-awareness leads to a willingness to change and adapt, and to be sensitive to others. It therefore helps when leading or working with a team.

I've interviewed hundreds of people over the years.

I've learned to ask the question differently. After I've asked about strengths I follow up with, "Those are useful personality traits. In what situations do you find those personality traits to be a disadvantage?"

This allows the candidate to talk openly about context. Personality traits usually have a positive side and a negative side. If your strengths are the heads side of a coin, don't forget that there's a tail on the other side of the same coin. Whether you see heads or tails depends on the way the coin is flipped.

Let's look at a simple example.

I took a Gallup strengths survey a few years ago. One of my strengths emerged as being a Maximiser.

The description of this strength included the following:

> "Taking something from below average to slightly above average takes a great deal of effort and in your opinion is not very rewarding. Transforming something strong into something superb takes just as much effort but is much more thrilling."

In the right job, in the right situation, that indeed is a strength. Equally, in certain situations, it can be a weakness. I can spend far too long on something that could have been done in half the time for the same impact.

In many ways our strengths are our weaknesses. It's the context that matters.

Are you great at being decisive and taking control? You're great in a crisis, but that could be a weakness if results are best achieved through collaboration.

This is a Yin-Yang view of personality.

If you are asked in an interview, "What are your weaknesses?", simply provide examples of situations where your strengths are not helpful to the tasks at hand.

If you're interviewing, try to understand the advantages and disadvantages of a candidate's strengths.

This way of thinking about strengths and weaknesses can also apply to companies. If you've ever done a SWOT (strengths, weaknesses, opportunities and threats) analysis, you may have noticed that very often a weakness is the opposite of a strength. For example, if your company is excellent at finding new customers through search engine marketing (a strength), this might be a weakness as the company becomes overly reliant upon search engines for its traffic. It may need to develop other marketing channels to complement search so that it's not exposed to a loss in new customers should the search engine change its algorithm.

Therefore, in order to identify weaknesses in a company, think about its strengths. In order to identify strengths, identify weaknesses - you may uncover a strength to exploit.

Amazon is an interesting example. Its weakness could be that it is reliant on third-party sellers. However, this provides a strength in that it maximises the range of products that it is able to offer. Another strength of Amazon's could be its strong brand awareness. This could lead to it being in the spotlight for regulatory issues (e.g. tax) more so than other companies, or a target for a cyber-attack, both of which could be potential weaknesses.

The paradox therefore is that if you want to find weaknesses, look for obvious strengths and think about the downside of those strengths.

Onboarding starts before onboarding

Think back to what it feels like to start a new job. You have a lot to take in.

I've had some fantastic experiences joining new teams. I've also had some poor experiences. The good experiences didn't happen by accident. Someone took care to make sure I had the tools and information I needed, introduced me to people, explained what was expected of me and helped me understand how to navigate my way around. Sometimes you don't know what you don't know and it's helpful to be given guidance on what you need to cover off.

Nine tips and tactics for onboarding new team members

1. Pre-starting:

- Invite the new person to join any team socials you have planned prior to their start so they can get to know people.
- See to it that the team the person will be joining sends its new starter a welcome email.
- Send over useful pre-reading material such as company history, customer research, company strategy or team objectives.
- Stay in touch on a regular basis until the new person joins. There's a risk that they could change their mind. It's a critical period.

2. The vision pitch:

- Early in the new starter's induction - and preferably in the first week - have the CEO/founder do a pitch session, selling the vision for the company. If there are external investors, the CEO should sell the same vision, so the new starter knows what expectations have been set.
- In high-growth situations (where new starters are joining every week), consider creating a weekly slot for the vision pitch, with all new starters who have joined that week attending.
- Either in this session or in a dedicated separate session, cover off company values and culture. If you can document this, even better.

3. The checklist:

- Have a living checklist of all the things that need to be covered in the onboarding plan. I say "living", because each time someone new starts, the previous checklist is updated.
- Use the following headers: Priority, Topic, Type, Who, Status. "Priority" can be simple: -1 = before starting; 0 = 1st day; 1 = 1st week; 2 = after that. "Topic" refers to the task (e.g. vision pitch with CEO or briefing

with sales team). "Type" could be things like software, HR, clients, office orientation and so on. "Who" would be the person who can help make this thing happen. "Status" tells you whether the task is "to do", "doing" or "done".

- Ensure the new starter owns their checklist and keeps it updated. If they need to book meetings or sessions, they should do it themselves. Getting people to run their own induction gives them ownership of their work and encourages self-sufficiency - very important in a startup.

- Consider the following items as examples to include for your checklist: set up email address; set up company phone (if applicable); set up laptop; invite to team social; complete new starter form; passport copy to HR; office orientation; P45 to HR; go through employment contract; meet key partners and clients; lunch with team in first week; set up 30-minute one-to-one intros with each member of the team; set up laptop, Wi-Fi, software and printer; send intro email to everyone in the company; set up email signature; change social media profiles; go through fire exit procedure; invite to team meetings; set up Google Drive/Dropbox; front door keys/security fob/alarm system; explain how post works; set up login for blog/Slack/Trello/other tools; introduction to vision/mission/strategy; go through company values and how we got there; go through docs on shared drive; update contact details on team directory; set up IM; buddy up; explain how to book meeting rooms; go through policies and procedures; read through staff handbook; set up weekly one-to-one with manager; write bio for website; get T-shirt and swag from [name]; update staff handbook (after one month); first-month feedback; and first-three-months feedback.

- There will be a lot of extra things you will add depending on the job role. What's key is to capture these every time you have a new joiner, so you don't forget them the next time.

4. The handbook:

- If you've got a new starter handbook, great. If not, start with a basic one.

- Ask each new starter to contribute to the new starter handbook after their first month. Correct any errors and add any new useful content.
- NB: This works well in small teams but is not so relevant once you're a mid-sized company.

5. The buddy:

- Having an allocated buddy who can show the ropes to your new starter can help with the onboarding experience.
- Sometimes there are small details that staff may not want to bother their manager with, and having a neutral peer to go to is good for quickly getting information, introductions or explanation of processes.

6. The feedback loop:

- Creating and maintaining an excellent onboarding experience requires continual iteration and tweaking. That means getting feedback on the process from new starters on a regular basis.
- If you can pre-schedule check-ins between the new starter and their manager, they are more likely to happen. In addition to scheduling weekly one-to-ones, schedule an onboarding/induction review after one day, one week, one month and three months (the three-month one being a probation confirmation, all being well).
- These meetings offer a chance to ask the new joiner how they are finding the induction, how much progress they've made on their checklist, what blockers there are and if there's anything the company can do to improve the onboarding experience.

7. The toolkit:

- Most companies use a variety of software tools, which are usually cloud based, and there are lots of logins to set up. Send all invites out ahead of time, so they're already in the new starter's inbox on day one.

- Likewise, send invites to any team meetings or future events so they're in the calendar from day one.
- Make sure that there's a desk, computer and screen ready for day one. If the new starter can walk in and get set up straight away, that makes for a better induction.

8. The welcome swag:

- If you have swag, put it on the new starter's desk on their first day before they arrive. T-shirts, stickers, branded notepads, mugs - whatever it is that you do, do it well on day one and give your new starter a little welcome pack.

9. The champion:

- To ensure consistently excellent onboarding, you need an onboarding champion. If you don't have an HR lead, then someone on the senior team needs to own it. Leaving each manager to their own devices will mean an inconsistent level of onboarding quality. The champion could be the COO, the Office Manager or the HR lead. As long as someone does it and does it well, the onboarding process will improve.
- The champion will have an onboarding planning meeting with the manager two weeks before the new starter joins (or ASAP in the case of a last-minute hire), they'll update the checklist and they'll make sure meetings are scheduled.

Chapter 2 - Organising the team

Delivering growth requires great teamwork. Having good players on the team is not enough to succeed - they need to play together to win. How team members work together to improve customer experience is an essential ingredient of success.

Average-player teams can beat star-player teams

I wasn't planning on jumping into the mountain lake.

Standing on the shore afterwards, I was surprised how warm I felt. It was a cold October day and it was drizzling. My feet were grounded on the stony shore and the icy rush that I had felt only a minute before was completely absent. I started to hear the laughter and cheers from my colleagues, who were as surprised as I was that I had stripped off my rain jacket, hiking boots and warm clothes to dash headfirst into the glacial water in my underwear. But it felt right, totally right.

We were at a secret location an hour or two from Verona in Italy. Mountain peaks surrounded us, and we had walked 15 kilometres to be at the lake. I was with my colleagues from the Holiday Extras leadership team. We'd traded our warm seaside office in Kent for the footpaths of the Italian hills for two days for a get-together focussed on becoming one team. But how? What is a good team? What could being in the outdoors teach us?

Just because a football team has the most expensive players, it doesn't mean they will win the championship. In fact, there are plenty of examples of smaller-budget teams beating those with a bigger payroll.

"The whole is greater than the sum of its parts." *Aristotle, b. 384 BC*

The same is true in business. But what is it about a team that makes it effective? Google researchers asked that question and published their findings in 2016. It makes for fascinating reading. Search for "Project Aristotle" and you'll find their report.

The research team found that there were several key ingredients for high-performing teams. Members of the team need to feel that their work has meaning and impact. There should be clear roles and goals to work to.

However, the most important factor, which underpins all the other success factors, is that the team have psychological safety. This means that team members feel safe to take risks and be vulnerable with each other. It means they trust each other. Trust is therefore the true foundation of teamwork.

All other things being equal, a team with higher psychological safety will outperform another team. Why is this?

In an environment of safety and trust, people are more willing to challenge each other, and say what needs to be said without fear of rejection. This helps foster a common understanding of the challenges faced and the ability to be creative around different ways to achieve the goal.

Back to the Italian hills. Our leadership team was on a short walking conference (I call it a talkabout or walkshop). The format was that we were posed a simple question that we were to consider and talk about whilst we walked. The first question was, "What is important to you about the team you work in/with?" I partnered with two or three different people over the first hour or so to discuss this topic, as did everyone else. It was fluid. The conversation took as long as it took and then we'd swap talking/walking partners whenever it suited. Walking side by side and looking in the same direction, we naturally talked as equals and with the same horizon, in our walking and in our talking.

As did Google in its research, we uncovered that trust was a common theme. To perform, we would need to encourage a culture of trust. And that, we realised, meant opening up to each other, being honest about how we were feeling and being true to ourselves. We agreed it was better to say "I don't know, I need help with this" than worry about losing face and pretending we knew the answer. Trust requires emotional safety and it requires accepting people for who they are so that they feel comfortable to share with you. To do this requires accepting yourself as being flawed and knowing your strengths and limits.

Our next question as we set off from the clearing was, "How do you get the best out of me?" We paired up, finding out how our colleagues liked and needed to work. This exercise required us to be honest and therefore to trust the other person. I remember explaining, for example, that I struggle to keep numbers in my head and so if I need to go to a meeting where we are going to talk metrics, I welcome advance warning so I can prepare my notes in advance. Someone else said they really needed to understand the "why" in any project and would want others to keep to the point and not confuse them with detail.

We regrouped at the top of a hill in a mossy clearing in the forest. Logs were moved into position to create a circle and one by one we shared how we like and need to work. I saw some real honesty in the group, which showed that we were starting to trust each other. I also saw intense listening as each person shared their needs. Respect for each other hung in the still forest air.

Our final question took us over the brow of the hill to a fantastic view, down the other side to a medieval village and onwards to the icy lake. It was, "What is your superpower?" In other words, the one thing that you're really good at, the special skill that you can bring to the team. Again, we discussed this in pairs, with different people, and started to recognise our strengths - our own and each other's. It sounds obvious, but knowing the special skills of your team members means you can ask for help when you need it and contribute when you can - a great basis for strong teamwork.

The superpowers were shared on a grassy knoll in front of the icy lake. They were funny, authentic and useful. At that moment I was intensely proud of the journey we'd taken on foot, and as a team.

That lake was cold. In my head a challenge had been set. Could I, would I, should I strip off and jump in, two months into a new job in front of a new team? I'm not sure where the idea came from but once it was there it wouldn't go away. I wasn't afraid of the cold or getting wet. The biggest barrier was whether I felt accepted by the team and if I trusted them. I told myself that if I really trusted them, they would accept me for being who I am - perhaps a little crazy and built like a stick. So I had to do it. Because I trusted them.

The warmth I felt on the beach afterwards was both physical and emotional. Physical because the air felt warm after being in icy water and emotional because I now truly felt part of a team.

We laughed about it together at dinner - a lovely evening in front of an ancient fireplace.

On the following morning we put our newly rebooted team skills to the test in a challenge set for us by the organisers. Theory on teamwork over, now it was time to practise. I saw a step change in how we communicated with each other following our learning from the previous day. We regrouped to reflect on our mini-adventure and the lessons learned. We vowed to bring the lessons from the mountains to the office. Then, we had a final lunch, thanked the organisers, and had to leave for the airport and head home, stronger, happier, exhausted and one team.

At the heart of it, great teamwork is founded on the willingness to be vulnerable and trust each other. This is something that researcher Brené Brown comes back to again and again. Her TED talk on the subject, "The Power of Vulnerability", is one of the most watched TED talks ever. (At the time of writing this it had over 60 million views - and if you haven't watched it, it's well worth 20 minutes of your time.)

As a leader, to execute on growth initiatives, you need a great team. You can set the culture of the team. And to be a truly great team, you need to be prepared to be open and vulnerable so that you are trusted. Trust is infectious. The more you open up, the more others will. As a leader, you go first and you set the tone. If you don't do it, it will be more difficult for others to do it.

So - find your lake and jump in feet first.

Capability requires both capacity and competence

Leaders contribute to setting the direction of the company - figuring out what direction to take and why (vision), as well as how to achieve it (strategy).

Therefore, Direction = Vision + Strategy

And for the company to be successful it needs to be capable to follow that direction.

Therefore, Success = Direction x Capability

Aside from setting direction, a leader needs to create and improve the capability of the company so that it can pursue its objectives effectively.

Digging deeper, capability has two main drivers: how much resource is available (capacity) and how skilled that resource is (competence).

Therefore, Capability = Competence x Capacity

Competence is how good we are at doing something and it's driven by four main factors: communication, skills, experience and information.

Capacity, however, is driven by how many resources we have (money, people or assets) and how productive or efficient we are with those resources.

Sometimes it is worth considering a growth challenge in terms of the capability you have at your disposal to work with. Or - if you need to improve your chances of success - think about which part of the equation needs work. Do you need to make the vision clearer? Do you have the right strategy? Do you need more resources? Do you need to focus on productivity? Do you need to improve communication flow? Or does the team need deeper experience? Do you upskill the team or hire in experience? Or - all of the above?

In summary, your ability to deliver as a team (your capability) is driven by both the capacity of the team and its competence.

Internal comms are no different to external comms

On a supermarket trip I was at the check-out. I saw the usual chewing gum, cooking magazines, batteries and chocolate on display - high-profit items that customers impulsively buy as they wait to pay for the rest of their goods. I wonder, if supermarkets had to rely on people only buying what they came to the shop to buy, would they actually make a profit at all?

Marketers have of course always understood that to generate a customer response they need to place the goods and services as close to the customer's existing path as they possibly can. The supermarket check-out is a classic example and has been taken to new extremes these days by almost every retailer. If I try and buy a bottle of water at the airport at the newsagent or chemist, I will inevitably meet with a queuing system that puts almost all the high-profit, impulsive-purchase products that the retailer has to offer in front of me whilst I wait for the next available check-out. Chocolates, crisps, sun cream, ear-plugs, travel pillows, tissues... The aim is to convert paying customers into higher-paying customers.

Google advertising has been so successful at generating traffic for companies because the potential customers are already there. Google knows the customers' intentions from their keywords and can offer companies the chance to place an ad in their existing path to sell products or services.

Likewise with TV advertising, to sell a home cleaning product to parents, you might place the advert on a kids TV channel, hoping they'd see it whilst they watch TV with their kids.

If you have a programme of change that you want to achieve in your organisation, think as a marketer would. They could think about distribution channels, paths and existing behaviours. Start thinking about internal comms in the same way as external comms. Who are my audience? Where can I reach them? How do I integrate my message into their existing behaviour? How can I get the results I want from their existing environment?

In a previous job, our tech team were trying to figure out how to build knowledge and awareness within the customer support team about how our products worked. Their solution, although commendable for the effort put in, was ineffective. They decided to create a standalone wiki where they would explain how things worked. New posts would be available by subscribing to a feed.

For this to succeed, all the customer support people needed to have a separate login for the wiki. Then, they all needed to configure their email client to pick up the feed. Then they needed to remember to check the feed folder in their inbox on a regular basis and read the articles. Sounded easy to the tech team. It failed.

Imagine if our supermarket had a separate room for all of its high-margin add-on sales. You had to go there specifically in order to see the product offerings. And you needed to pick up a separate basket in order to carry these products to the check-out in addition to your main trolley. They wouldn't sell anything, would they?

Using the path most travelled is why the supermarket check-out system works for the add-on sales. Using the path least travelled is the reason why the tech wiki failed.

For the tech wiki project to work, it needed to use the systems that the customer support staff were already using on a daily basis. There were three: the company's back-office system, the CRM database and email inboxes. Anything outside of these three systems was irrelevant because support staff were too busy dealing with these three systems to think about adding another.

So, when trying to introduce a change to an organisation, focus on making your change happen using existing pathways. Making change happen is hard enough. Having to create new pathways at the same time makes it even harder.

As a bonus, not only is the path most travelled the easiest place to introduce your change, it's also the path of least resistance.

No matter what their discipline or function, the more that managers think like marketers, the more likely they are to succeed. Be where people are and be where they are receptive.

Find and use the path most travelled.

Innovation comes in many flavours

It turns out that we all have different ways of innovating. If you can identify your default style, you can use it to your advantage by putting yourself into situations where that style is most useful. And if you're an entrepreneur or work with entrepreneurs, you're going to be innovating a lot - how you do so is determined by your style.

When my daughter was six, she wanted us to play Lego together.

We had a big box of Lego, the result of several years of mashing up pieces from lots of different gifts. Some of it is handed down. It had a bit of everything.

"Daddy, please can you build me a zoo?" she asked.

Now there's a challenge. I could remember that we had two Lego crocodiles but other than that we had no zoo set to build from. We were going to have to build it from whatever we could find.

With the challenge set, we first set about finding every single green piece we could find, plus some browns. (After all, we figured zoos are mainly natural colours.)

Then we started building. I had no idea how this zoo would turn out. It was simply a case of experimenting with a few base pieces and building, tinkering as we went. It was fun. My daughter made a wolf and found a parrot to go with the crocodiles.

Given our resources, I was surprised and pleased with the end result. My daughter was very happy and modified the resulting structure to reflect her own personality, adding odd pieces here and there.

What we didn't do was imagine/envision and architect a master plan before we started. We just got started and figured it out as we went. Nor did we modify an existing structure. We just had a go. We tested, iterated and learned as we went.

The four styles of innovation

Around that time, a friend had been talking about a training course he'd been on at work where they explored the four styles of innovation (see Debra Miller's 2007 overview):

- Exploring

- Visioning
- Modifying
- Experimenting

Styles are determined from two main dimensions...

Are you stimulated and inspired to innovate by:

- facts, details and analysis, or
- intuition, insights and images?

And do you approach innovation in a way that is:

- focussed, well planned and outcome oriented, or
- broad, perceptive and learning oriented?

My experimental style is a combination of being inspired by facts, details and analysis and approaching innovation from a broad, perceptive, learning-oriented angle.

This insight was helpful. It made me realise that I am weakest at envisioning the future but strongest at figuring out how to get there. That means my ideal job is one where I partner with a visionary person who has imagined what the future could be, and I help figure out how to get there. I'm not so much of a visionary. I look at the resources I have and go figure what I could make from them. I try stuff out. I have a go.

It turns out that this has been the signature of my career to date: getting stuck into the detail of how, working in early-stage organisations that have strong visions with a large appetite for change. It also explains why I'm drawn to lean startup methods (test, iterate and learn).

Implications for entrepreneurs

If we accept that there are different styles of innovation, we can start to think about what types of environments suit these different styles.

(Everyone has their own unique blend of styles and it's probable that they'll have a dominant one. This isn't a simple binary framework. Like all models, it will have some fluidity when applied to real life.)

All four types of innovation style have value:

- Some projects would not come to exist without the imagination of their creator. New markets are made possible by those who imagine them to be. These are the visionaries with bold ideas disrupting the world. Uber, perhaps?
- Some opportunities are found by modifying an existing business model and launching in an adjacent sector or market. These are the modifiers. Rocket Internet, perhaps?
- Sometimes it's a question of exploring new forms of technology and then, once found, finding a great application for them. These are the explorers. Maybe an example of this is when Steve Jobs visited Xerox PARC, found a computer mouse and saw that it had a great future in personal computing.
- Then, there are the times when you just start with a small concept and test it, find something that works and then keep building. These are the experimenters. Twitter (X) started this way.

So you see - if we know our own style, we can all innovate, in our own way. We all complement each other and strong teams will have a mixture of styles.

Ask yourself, if you play with Lego, how do you build?

The size of your team determines how it will behave

150 - the magic number

Do organisational structures need to transform once they exceed 150 members in number?

Many companies experience growth that takes them past the 150-team member mark without them realising what's happening to them.

Why 150? What is it with 150 that makes it significant?

The idea was first floated by British anthropologist Robin Dunbar (b. 1947), but subsequently popularised by Malcolm Gladwell in his book *The Tipping Point*.

Known as Dunbar's number, 150 is the theoretical maximum group size in which individual members all know and can maintain social relationships with each other.

Once you cross the threshold from being a small company to a larger one, the old ways just don't work any more. You need a different way of managing communication, direction and decision making. What's more, the people who worked well in the old environment probably aren't the same type of people who work well in a bigger team. "Things aren't the same around here", "It's not what it used to be" - suddenly you've got 30% attrition and a stressed-out recruitment team.

I once read that W. L. Gore & Associates (makers of Gore-Tex, among other things) keep the size of manufacturing teams under 150 people. It has found this size keeps people in touch with each other. If it needs more production capacity, rather than expand a team that's at the 150 limit, it'll start a new one.

Army regiments work in a similar manner. And just for good measure, Dunbar's surveys of settlements in ancient times show they also tended to be limited to about 150 people.

Good companies require effective teams to succeed. Most companies however grow organically and rarely do leaders stop and ask how the social relationships in their teams work and how growth might affect those relationships.

Complexity of groups is exponential

People often ask me what it's like to have four kids. The answer is, it's fantastic. Another point I make though is that a six-person family is exponentially more complex than a four-person family. Here's why.

When you first meet your partner, there is one relationship. Two people with one relationship.

If you then have a child, there are now three relationships. Parent 1 < > Parent 2, Parent 1 < > Child, Parent 2 < > Child.

In a family of four, there are six relationships. In a family of six however the number of relationships rockets. To 15!

Our family mealtimes can have up to 15 different possible interactions going on. Everyone has to work harder to be heard and needs to be able to listen and wait their turn to talk.

It's like this in startups. The more people you add, the more relationships are added, and most people don't realise that the complexity is non-linear.

So what happens when you get to 50 people?

As it happens, there's a formula to work out the number of potential relationships. Where r is the number of potential one-to-one relationships and n is group size, the formula is this:

$$r = (n \times (n-1)) / 2$$

50 people gives the following result:

(50 [group size] x 49 [group size minus one]) / 2 = 1225 [potential relationships]

1225 potential relationships!

Tripling from 50 people to 150 can increase complexity not three-fold but 10-fold! That's 10 times as many possible relationships.

Humans typically deal with the increasing complexity by creating more formal communication and relationship structures, the most common one being a hierarchy.

Just as Dunbar's number is an inflection point in terms of the complexity of human groups, there are other inflection points to be aware of. An inflection point can be considered a turning point, after which a dramatic change, with either positive or negative results, is expected to occur.

"It all changes when you get to 50 people", Alicia Navarro, then CEO of Skimlinks, said at a talk she gave about startup growing pains. She's right - in my experience, what you do to manage a team of 30 people is very different to what you do when you manage a team of 60. And 50 is a number that matters. It's an inflection point.

I've seen this myself. At Bookatable we grew from 25 people to 170 people in three years. At HouseTrip we grew from eight people to 160 people in less than two years. I've worked in teams of all sizes - ranging from those with fewer than 10 members to larger companies with more than 2,000 people.

On each growth journey there were inflection points caused by the number of people in the company.

I've found that there are three company-size inflection points that startups need to be aware of.

Whenever the organisation size goes past one of these numbers, the dynamics change. What worked before doesn't work now. Different skills, processes and leadership styles are needed.

You might find that you thrive in one group size but struggle in another. This is totally normal, and most people don't realise that the group size itself has a massive effect on what's needed to survive and thrive as a contributor or leader.

People who join a startup when it's at 15 people sometimes find they don't like the way things are changing when they get to 150 - or even 50 - people. They miss out on information, they are not included in as many decisions, there are process hoops to jump through and they just don't like it. This is normal.

Many people don't realise that you can predict how human groups will behave depending on how large they are. And because fast-growing startups (or scale-ups) can grow every month, the dynamic changes without anyone noticing. Unless, of course, you know these inflection points exist - and that they matter.

It's my opinion that team dynamics in scale-ups change in a predictable way. I use the analogy of human settlement sizes to illustrate what I mean. I'll list them below. This is the default progression that most teams will see unless they do something to the contrary. There are predictable inflection points where the team dynamics change.

The three inflection points; 7, 50, 150

There's also a third inflection point to be aware of that happens very early in the startup journey: seven people. Seven, 50 and 150 - any time the group size increases (or decreases) past these thresholds, everything changes, and nobody realises!

Many companies start with a single founder. There is no group here so there is no group dynamic - just one person trying to do everything and wishing there were more hours in the day.

Then, there is a team...

2-7 people - The Hunting Party

In this small group size, it's as if there is a hunt.

Imagine our ancestors out for the day tracking deer on foot. The group works together in real time with some planning (but only where needed). A leader often emerges, but really only if someone needs to be in charge and if people are willing for that person to be the leader.

Everyone has their own skills and contribution. Everyone is involved and everyone knows almost everything. The team has an objective to catch its prey, and members work together on this common purpose using the skills and tools they have at their disposal.

8-50 people - Family Huts

When the hunting party brings back its prey, it's to a small settlement with a few huts, one for each family. Each family has a recognised leader who's there if required, but most people still talk directly to each other and everyone is on first-name terms with each other. The elders might tell stories around the fireplace in the evening and not much organisation is required.

This is what the early stage of a startup is like once you get past seven people. There are distinctive groups that take on specific responsibilities and challenges - the tech team, the sales team, the marketing team, etc. You need leaders for each group, but very little process is needed, and work gets done, albeit chaotically.

50-150 people - The Village

As Skimlinks' Alicia Navarro said, once you get past 50 people, everything changes.

You now have to work at it so that people bond. You need to start developing processes to get stuff done. You try to channel communications. You have to broadcast more information. You start having to channel requests and instructions via group leaders. You have a more formal decision-making leadership team.

You now have a light hierarchy.

This is like a small village. In a small village there are specialist roles: the schoolteacher, the bar owner, the mechanic, and so on. There are people in charge and there are more rules. You can still know everyone, what their role is and how they relate to each other, but you won't be on first-name terms with everyone.

150+ people - The Town

After 150 (*Dunbar's 150*), the village becomes a town.

Here, it becomes almost impossible to know everyone by name and to know what everyone does. Throughout history, humans have defaulted to a hierarchy system to organise themselves in larger groups. There are probably many exceptions, but it is very common to use hierarchy as an effective organisational method.

In the town there are systems. These make sure that repeated and expected events are handled with predictability. There are traffic lights, drainage systems, planning restrictions and street numbers. There are people in charge and there are people who work within more specialist roles.

So, in a group of 150, it is still possible to know everyone else and understand their roles and their relationships with each other. Beyond that, forget it. This number, like seven and 50, is pretty significant therefore when it comes to shaping organisational structures. With a team of 150, you can still manage with a relatively flat reporting structure, and fairly informal communication and decision-making processes.

Every company that scales will face these challenges. All fast-growing teams will experience similar organisational challenges as they reach and pass the inflection points.

Think about your own preferences and where you thrive.

Some CEOs that launch startups can really struggle in a big organisation. Some big company CEOs would struggle to launch a startup from scratch. We all have our sweet spot.

I've learned over the years that I am suited to "family huts" and "village" life.

I can hunt if I need to, and I prefer not to be a townie (although I'm learning a new set of skills to perform better in larger groups). At heart, I'm more of a village dweller. That's where my skills are best used. It suits my management style, partly because I like to do, and partly because you need more political skill to succeed in town and less so in the village.

Whatever your preference, pay attention to group size and what it does to your culture - you underestimate it at your peril.

Do more with fewer people

If a new manager were to approach me early in their career and ask today, "David, how can I really manage workflow well?", I'd give them the following 10 tips. They are what I aspire to myself every day.

Whether it's managing software development teams, call centres, HR projects or events, I've found these principles to work. Reading about Japanese production methodologies has helped me reflect on what has worked for me and why.

If done well, you can actually achieve more with fewer people.

So, here are my 10 tips for getting stuff done well.

1. Make the workflow public

Get the work on the wall. In real time.

These days there are plenty of software solutions to track the status of a project but sadly even the best software can sometimes fail when it comes to improving team effectiveness. For teams working across different locations, software is very useful. However, for teams working at the same location, it can be more effective to put the work progress on the wall.

I once had to rally my team to reduce our customer service backlog in our service centre. I put the number of outstanding tickets (issues) up as a big number at the entrance to the room and updated it every hour. I also set a target that we needed to hit by the end of the week. That way I knew everybody on the team would see the progress we were making and understood the importance and urgency. If I had created an online dashboard I could not have been sure that everyone would see it on a regular basis.

Displaying progress at a computer screen is not a public act. Displaying progress in a public area creates peer pressure and fosters accountability. If you know your work progress is made public, you are more likely to do your best to hit your targets.

Simply getting the status of the project on a wall and updating it on a daily basis creates awareness amongst all team members and prompts discussions such as, "Why is everything stuck in the design phase?", "We're not going to hit our target, so what are we going to do?" or "We're doing well." For example, use sticky notes that represent tasks that move along between phases of a project, columns for these phases and rows for individuals or sub-teams. Or, in the case of service environments, create categories such as "open cases today", "calls waiting" or "calls successfully answered within three rings".

By making the data public and keeping it updated, the team starts to work together to address the challenge.

You might think that sticky notes and whiteboards are an extra layer of information processing that you don't need if you already track on a computer. Even if there is an extra cost for maintaining real-time analogue information, I've found the productivity gains to be worth the extra effort. It's counterintuitive but, like most things counterintuitive, it has a surprising effect.

Visual controls - they're very, very effective.

2. Go and see the work

You can run all the metrics you like but a good manager needs to be close to the work.

If you're a senior manager, this is not practical to do with all the teams that you manage, but you still need to periodically go and see and literally spend time observing. It's these observations (supported by relevant data) that allow you to make smart decisions. What's important to fix right now? What's causing the delay/error/problem? Who can help me improve this situation?

A manager is focussed on what's closest to them. So go to where your customers are and you'll end up focussing on your customers.

3. Be your own customer

I use the word "customer" in the very broadest sense. It can refer to a consumer (a purchaser of the product or service), a supplier or a colleague in another team. Basically, if you deliver value to anyone, internally or externally, they are your customer.

For example, the finance team are customers of the HR team because they require payroll data from the HR team. The worker getting paid at the end of the month is the customer of the finance team.

By being your own customer you can experience what it is like to be a customer. What problem is it that you need solved? What does it feel like to have that problem solved by your company? What could be better and why?

People pay for products and services to solve a problem that they have - for example, around communication (telephone), keeping in touch with friends (social network), self-esteem (fashion), hunger (food) or family time (holiday).

If you don't experience the problem and solution yourself, you cannot achieve the same level of understanding. Go and be your own customer, and experience your products or services as a customer would. That helps you to see the value and see the improvements needed.

4. Be able to do the work yourself

Just sitting among a team creates an awareness that you can't get by sitting in an office next door. Even better, having done the work yourself enables you to truly appreciate what could be improved.

If you shadow a team member for a day or two, see what it's like to receive the information that they receive and use the tools that they use. You will be so much more aware of what's important, possible or needed.

Some of the very best managers are those who worked their way up through the organisation, so know the work in detail from the ground up. They are indeed grounded, yet have managed to take on senior manager roles. This gives them the ability to have both a helicopter view (seeing the big picture, a leadership perspective) and a ground-level view (the challenges of executing against a plan). And they can switch between the two quickly and at will.

This is why it's so important to develop people within a team and train the next generation of leaders from within if at all possible.

5. Reduce work in progress

This is one of the most important and effective principles of all and it's one of the most difficult to implement. We often hear about the importance of focus. Focus is all about deciding what not to do rather than what to do. It is actually about reducing work in progress.

If you have 10 tasks that you are working on simultaneously, you will switch between tasks a lot. If you have two or three tasks, you can generally work through them in some detail and do them properly. You will actually end up doing more and doing it better. Fact. Trust me.

Easy to say, not easy to do. Why?

Take email as an example. You have a number of projects on the go. You send and reply to emails, and that's often because you're collaborating with others to achieve a project goal. Rarely do we work completely alone. The emails that are sent go out into the world and one day they might come back with the information you need, and you can carry on. In the meantime, what do we do? We go to meetings and collect new to-do actions, plus we reply to whatever is in our inbox. This creates more threads and open items. Everyone else you're working with is doing the same thing. And before long, the organisation is multitasking and task-switching, adding more and more tasks that take longer and sometimes aren't finished at all.

To combat this, discipline is needed. One way to achieve this is to periodically meet as a work group (daily or weekly, depending on the group) and identify the top three things that matter for the period. Then work together on those first three things - not 10 things, three things - every day until they're done.

And importantly, do not start anything new unless you've finished what you can on those three things.

You can always create a queue to have agreed items next in line once you have spare capacity to pull new work onto your schedule.

If you force a limit on the number of items in progress at any one time, the ones in progress move faster and the overall speed of the team improves.

6. Document the process

By writing down your process you have a point from which to measure and optimise it. In fact I would argue that the main purpose of documenting a process is so that you can change it in the future.

The process of documentation (whether it be in words or diagrams) exposes the process to the eyes of the team. You can start to see opportunities to optimise it. Do we really need to do that bit? If we bypassed step 4, would it speed up the process? How many people are involved, and could we reduce that? (See point 10.)

Go back to the process on a regular basis and ask, "How can we make this process better for our customers?"

Once a team understands that a process is there to be changed and not to be blindly followed without critiquing, it can be very empowering.

7. Measure the flow

How long does it take for a task to go from initiation to completion? Measuring the speed of work but also the variance of work demand is essential to speed up and smooth out the flow. And speeding up and smoothing out the flow (see point 9) leads to better value for all involved.

An example for an HR team: from job requisition approved to offer made, what is our average lead-in time? (And, following on from that, what causes the delay in the process and how do we improve that without reducing the quality of hires?) If you can measure the flow, you can improve it. So go figure out how to measure.

8. Design processes starting with the customer

In any system, there is some kind of end result. Software shipped. Employee hired. Customer enquiry answered. Expenses paid.

When designing processes, start with the end customer (either internal or external) and figure out who sits directly before them in the process. Then who sits before them. And so on. The end customer is downstream of the process and the initiator of the process is upstream. Think of a process as a river system. Some parts of the system feed others and so upstream and downstream describe the relative positions of parts of a process.

I like to think about processes by starting with the end of the process - the part closest to the customer. If there are several people involved in delivering a product or service, the process needs to be designed so that the downstream people get what they need when they need it. Then work backwards.

This is known as a pull system. A true pull system provides the quickest path to providing value for the customer.

So many organisations and teams work the other way around. They push things through and you end up with bottlenecks, delays and stress.

This is a really tricky principle to pull off well and making it happen requires the buy-in of decision makers involved. I can't claim to have mastered this myself in all areas of my work. I have however seen it work very well in software development teams that I've managed.

9. Level the flow

What does levelling the flow mean?

In software it means a steady stream of (pulled) productive work without overloading the team with spikes of (pushed) deadlines.

In contact centres levelling the flow means predicting inbound consumer demand and matching staffing schedules to meet those predicted demands rather than being quiet on slow days/hours and overwhelmed on busy days.

Sometimes you'll pull ahead of demand, sometime you'll catch up but all the while your people are steadily adding value in a productive way.

10. Reduce the number of people involved in a task

If a task has two people involved and four steps it will be much faster than if there are four people and four steps.

If a task has two people involved and four steps it will be faster than if there are two people and six steps.

Reducing the steps and the people increases speed and, as long as quality is not decreased, increases value.

Modern companies tend to evolve to create division of labour. This is very useful, in fact. A lawyer is better at being a lawyer than a software developer and vice versa. So for some tasks you need experts. But for others there can be a division of labour, because it's easier to train one person to do one thing than train one person to do many things. Plus, you can pay less for the low-value tasks.

So, a simple question to ask is "Do I really need this division of labour for this task, or do I just need to invest in training?"

As customers we hate being passed from one person to another. So as business owners we need to do that only when needed and create a multi-talented, well-trained team.

Under-optimise a system and it will run faster

Would you run a train network at 100% passenger capacity all the time? No, I don't think you would. There's no slack. If one problem occurs, there's no room to manoeuvre. There'd be a crisis. A meltdown.

In fact, that's one of the problems with London's Heathrow Airport. It runs at 97-98% capacity. Most of the available take-off and landing slots are being used most of the time. When bad weather hits, big delays ramp up quickly unless some scheduled flights are cancelled.

So, it stands to reason that as managers we shouldn't try and run our people at 100%. If we do, a crisis will easily happen. We'll then be firefighting instead of growing.

Or maybe not. The counter view is this: if we are running at less than 100%, we are doing everything with time to spare. Some of that work is less important than the rest. If we say no to things, let's say no to the least important things. If you're saying yes to everything, you're not prioritising.

One way to navigate this dilemma is to make a distinction as follows.

Does all the work have to happen within a fixed time frame? Or not?

Predictable fixed tasks with defined time frames - these are best run with some slack capacity to allow for unforeseen circumstances.

Transport and logistics would fit this model. Or fixed-deadline civil engineering projects.

Unpredictable tasks with non-defined time frames are best queued in order of priority. They can then be worked through at 100% capacity, taking a new task from the top of the list as soon as another is completed. If there's a problem, simply pause until the problem is dealt with and then get back to the high-priority work.

Software development and creative work might fit better with this model.

There's no right and wrong here. I'm just highlighting that there are benefits to running with slack and benefits to running with no slack.

Ultimately, it boils down to a simple question: "What will happen if we can't complete this by a certain time?"

As a startup you're usually running at way above capacity simply because the answer to that question is the amount of cash you have left. At some point however you might need to design slack in your system to avoid a crisis.

Chapter 3 - Team performance

As a leader, driving performance from a team is more than setting objectives and creating systems and structures. A big contributing factor is motivation and how you act as a leader to create a high-performance culture.

Fast feedback is better than slow feedback

The legendary soul sensation James Brown had an incredible stage presence.

He was known to dance with his back to the audience, sliding across the stage as if he were conducting his band. The audience thought this was part of the act and few realised what was going on.

The hand signals he flashed to his band with a splayed hand were not a high-five. He was signing "$5" to a particular member of the band. $5 was his fine for musicians when he heard a wrong note or noticed dirty shoes. Each pulse of Brown's hand was a $5 fine; five pulses would mean a fine of

$25.

If you look carefully, I'm sure you can see the musicians' faces drop as they receive the signals.

There's a lesson here for all of us: feedback loops are more effective the sooner you give the feedback.

In a concert, Brown couldn't afford to wait until the end of the show to give feedback. If someone was out of time, he needed correction immediately.

This idea of giving quick feedback was popularised in best-selling book *The One Minute Manager* by Kenneth Blanchard. I read the book about 25 years ago. The one thing I remember was that giving feedback as soon as an action has happened helps both the person receiving the feedback and the person giving it. This applies equally for both praise and criticism.

You know if you're on the right track. If you're not, you know your manager will tell you so you can do something about it. No nasty surprises waiting for you at the next quarterly (or annual) review meeting.

I also think this lesson applies to growth projects.

First, customer feedback needs to be gathered quickly.

This applies at all stages of a company. The quicker that feedback can be gathered and understood from customers, the faster are the learning cycles that can drive change and improvement.

Second, keep projects on track with regular and quick updates.

A great example of short feedback loops is the daily stand-up meeting favoured by agile software development teams.

Things move fast in business. They have to - it costs money to develop a business.

The "Godfather of Soul" (James Brown) reminds us that when time is of the essence, give real-time feedback when you can.

Ask for either more of the same, or more, or less

Here's a simple way of giving and receiving one-to-one feedback.

Schedule a time and ask your team member to come ready to answer these three questions (thinking about how they do their job):

- What could you do more of?
- What could you do less of?
- What could you continue to do the same?

You can also ask them to be ready to answer these additional questions (thinking about how you manage them):

- As your manager, what could I do more of?
- As your manager, what could I do less of?
- As your manager, what could I continue to do the same?

For your own preparation, also ask yourself the following questions.

About your own performance as a manager (thinking about how you manage them):

- As a manager, what could I do more of?
- As a manager, what could I do less of?
- As a manager, what could I continue to do the same?

About your team member (thinking about how they do their job)

- What could they do more of?
- What could they do less of?
- What could they continue to do the same?

I've used this structure on a few occasions and it's a super easy way to have constructive conversations.

It's two way

If you're prepared to give feedback, be prepared to receive it. This creates a more open and honest discussion. It's also a great chance to learn how you could do things differently to be more effective.

Could versus should

"Could" is suggestive. "Should" is judgemental. I used "could" for the things we might consider changing. These are discussion points, not pronouncements. People are more receptive to suggestions than judgements.

Preparation is key. It's difficult to have this discussion without thinking about it first.

Praise gets included

Some of these questions - especially the "more of" and "continue the same" ones - are great for praising great performance. Even the "less of" questions can be used for constructive comment.

Try it out yourself. It's the simplest feedback structure I know yet incredibly useful.

You can crowdsource motivation

You want to say "well done" more to your team?

I know I do. However, I'm just not a gushing type. Every management course I've ever been on emphasises the need to praise, to recognise, to make people feel valued - the idea being that feeling valued is motivational and sustains a team.

Essentially, you want your team to do a good job. Giving praise is only a tiny part of that equation though. For some people, praise is their fuel, their driving force. Praise them and they'll do anything. For others, it's not so simple. Sure, I like to be told I'm doing a good job. Who doesn't? But does it get me out of bed in the morning? Nope. For me it's all about being engaged. Being engaged in what you're doing and feeling that your effort has some real value. Being engaged, plus doing every day what you do best. Learning new tricks and solving challenges, that's good too. Oh yeah - and a "well done" afterwards is a good bonus. Did I mention the money?

Anyway, you see my point - praise isn't the magic ingredient in management. It's not going to do much if all the other motivational factors are not in play. It's the icing on the cake. (Except for the few people who get so high on praise that it's their wonder drug - give them praise and it will be like a turbo charge.)

It's hard to praise well. For me this is because firstly, the person needs to feel like they deserve the praise and secondly, the best praise is delivered in front of others. Tricky.

So, here's my idea. I've tried it out and it seems to work.

At the beginning of your team meeting, ask each team member to write up on a white board or flip chart one thing that they, the team or another team member did well last week and which helped them work towards achieving their objectives.

It's great! Team members write up on the board things they know are worth highlighting. They are happy enough that these achievements are worthy of praise. So, problem one is solved and the person feels the achievement was praiseworthy.

Often, team members will highlight things that they have done that aren't actual deliverables but are changes to the way in which the team works together. This is good, because it highlights process optimisation, communication and/or infrastructure improvements.

On other occasions they might highlight softer things like new starters joining the team.

And sometimes they praise each other rather than themselves. A double whammy - public and peer praise.

One interesting thing about this technique is that the team is creating a sense of positive behavioural reinforcement. By writing the achievement on the wall, they are committing themselves to a viewpoint that this achievement was a good thing. Writing something down commits the person in a very strong way to continuing to behave in the same way in the future. It helps form their identity.

The process is unusual. By adopting it, the team creates a ritual that is a way to mark themselves out from other teams. Although it's not a big deal, it's an act that team members share that others don't. So it strengthens the team identity, and it does so in a positive context.

Once everyone has had a go (I would go last), I then ask each team member to write on a sticky note the item that they think was the best achievement of the week. We post the notes together on the wall at the same time. Usually one achievement stands out and I can then spend a few moments praising that effort in front of the whole team.

With everyone in a good mood and in team mode, we then set about tackling the rest of the agenda.

Saying well done has never been so easy or so much fun!

Give your team the V

Twenty-plus years ago I used to row. It's an amazing sport which requires intense dedication. But when it comes together, the feeling is amazing. Eight crew and the cox in a boat, moving in perfect harmony in 3D, powering the boat with finesse so it planes over the surface of the water. It's possibly the ultimate team sport. If one person doesn't show up, you can't take the boat out. If one person doesn't train as hard, they are carried by everyone else.

Great teams achieve more together than they could alone.

Geese know this. In a BBC news article titled "Fly like a bird: The V formation finally explained", I read:

> "Scientists say they have solved the mystery of why birds fly in a V formation, by tracking critically endangered birds that were being trained to migrate."

This wasn't news to me. Our rowing coach had told us about the V formation of flying geese as a way to explain to us what real teamwork was. The birds take it in turns to fly in the front. This is because the other birds can benefit by flying in the slipstream of the front bird. One bird works hard so the others can save energy. Then they switch. By doing this, they all use less energy than flying straight into the wind all the time.

It's the same for cyclists. If you watch the Tour de France or any other pro cycling race, you'll see that the team leaders are supported by their team. The leaders save their energy for the big finish of the day by riding in the slipstream of their teammates (riding in a slipstream can reduce the energy required to keep pace by as much as 40%), and their teams do the hard work to get them close to the finish with as much energy left as possible. The team leader finishes the job. In cycling, even on Sunday club rides, each rider is expected to take their turn at the front and dig hard and deep for a few minutes before returning to the slipstream of the bunch. By doing this, the speed of the group increases overall.

Needless to say, there are lots of lessons to be learned here for how we can be a great team together at work. It's fairly obvious, but here are some takeaways:

- Take turns at the front.
- Share the effort.
- Dig deep when it's your turn.
- Stay together.
- Head in the same direction.

Improve your ask, say why

You're in a queue to buy a train ticket. If you don't buy your ticket in the next three minutes you will miss your train. You need to find a way to be served next.

Which of these would most likely get you a place at the front of the queue?

1. "Please could I jump the queue and go before you?"
2. "I'm about to miss my train. Please could I jump the queue and go before you?"
3. "If I don't get this train, I'm going to be late for an interview that could

change my life. Please could I jump the queue and go before you?"

Naturally, 3 will work better than 2, and 2 will work better than 1.

It's simple. If you need something from someone, you can improve your chances of success massively if you explain why.

It's a wonder why so many people forget this when they get to work. I think it's because in the examples above we are relying purely on a social exchange to get what we need. At work, we are in a transactional environment, people are being paid to do what other people ask, and hierarchy and power plays interfere. This means we sometimes get lazy with our asks.

Give someone a reason to do something and they'll be more likely to do it.

If you knew you couldn't fail, what would you do?

I'm lucky to have four kids. I didn't teach them to walk. They didn't teach each other. They just got up and had a go. First of all they started to figure out how to pull themselves up to stand against the furniture. Then they took one or two steps. A few weeks later they were walking.

We all first learnt by trial and error.

Later in childhood, we start to learn from others. We are taught. We go to school. At the age of six it was quite amazing to have my eldest daughter read a book to me. Six months earlier, she couldn't read.

We are taught.

There's a third phase. Once we know how things work, we can go figure things out for ourselves. Some kids spend hours playing tennis, some spend hours programming and others spend hours and hours making things. Some of these kids will become the best in the world at what they do - literally the best in the world. In this phase, we practise. We seek guidance and we practise some more. We put hours and hours in. We make mistakes and learn from them. We practise some more.

We are self-taught and we practise.

But then we become adults. Some people continue with trial and error. It's called "learning on the job" in the business world. Some are taught. It's called "training" in the business world. Some practise, work long, hard hours, push themselves and become the best in the world at what they do. I'm not sure what we call these people, but I admire them.

I am more thirsty for knowledge now than I have ever been in my life. The more I learn, the more I realise there is to learn. And I want to be the best in the world at what I do. Why? It's simple. There's very little in life that beats the feeling you get when you say "Today I did what I do best!"

Today I aim to do what I do best. Will you?

Imagine a team where every person can say that. Can you imagine what that team would be able to achieve? It would be extraordinary. World beating. In fact just writing this makes my hair stand on end - it really is something special. It's like watching the Oxford Cambridge Boat Race and seeing the winners win. It's awesome.

The thing about great teams is one plus one equals three. The sum of the parts is greater than the whole. Only it's not guaranteed. Sometimes two egotistical geniuses equal less than two, because they haven't figured out how to collaborate well.

So on a practical note, how do we build great teams where every person does what they do best and on top of that build a winning team?

How do we make that team possible?

Here are the six main ingredients:

1. Allow people to make mistakes

If we make more mistakes, we learn more. I'm not saying that we should aim to fail. Rather, we should always be "doing". Doing something means you have the opportunity to learn. If you don't do anything, you won't make any mistakes, but then again you won't learn anything. This is the thinking behind the phrase *"fail faster"*. It's not that you should aim to fail. Instead, you *should do more faster* - because that's how you'll learn.

Fear holds us back though. We are afraid to make mistakes in case we are not seen as successful by our peers (and our own egos).

My wife and I were talking about why she is successful at what she does. She does business development, and she needs to figure out how to book meetings with managers and then persuade them to use her firm's services. She said that you can't book meetings without making phone calls, so she has to be very persistent to keep calling until she gets the meeting. She will keep calling long after other people have given up. Most people fear rejection, whereas she doesn't.

Her motto is "If you knew you wouldn't fail, what would you do?" Great advice indeed.

So, as a manager, I will always say to my team, "Make decisions and do stuff. Better to do lots and be right 95% of the time than to do a little and be right 100% of the time. You'll learn faster and so will I."

2. Trust your colleagues and help them learn from their mistakes

You can only build a truly successful team if there is true openness. I need to be open with my intentions, emotions and reasoning. This means my colleagues can help me identify what I'm doing well and what I can do better, and I will learn faster. If I do this though, I am opening myself up. I am doing exactly the opposite of what most people do in business. It requires mutual trust, respect and willingness - and it needs to start at the top.

3. Design learning structures

A great example of this is how we used to run our software development cycles in one of my previous companies. We planned our work in two-week cycles. This was pretty effective in terms of getting things done. The important ingredient I think that actually made it successful was that after every cycle ("sprint") we set up a "retrospective meeting". This was a simple meeting where we simply asked, "What went well, what didn't go so well and how will we in future do more of the good stuff and less of the bad stuff?" Doing this systematically requires a regular meeting slot in the diary, an agenda and a habit. It requires structure.

Good teams create these structures consciously to become learning teams.

4. Hire people who can handle this culture

This is critical. If you believe that you want to build world-class winning teams, you need to hire accordingly. Sure, you need talent and experience. I say they're overrated.

Just because someone has knowledge and the ingredients to make a great cake, it doesn't mean that they will. And just because someone was motivated to bake great cakes in the past doesn't mean that they will do so again in a different kitchen.

The questions that matter are:

- Does this person know how to apply themselves to a challenge?
- Is this person willing to open themselves up and be fully transparent with their emotions, reasoning and intentions?
- Are they able to give feedback to others in a helpful way?
- Are they thirsty to be the best in the world at something?

5. Go with the flow

You cannot tell people what motivates them. In my experience, people do best at what they are interested in, not necessarily what they are good at. I might be quite good at filing and organising paperwork. It doesn't mean I'm interested in it. Give me a reason to be interested in it, or find me something to do in which I will be interested, and I will do it well. Really well.

As people develop in your team, find opportunities for them and help them where possible to grow in your organisation to do what they do best. Build the team around the capabilities you have and seek out new team members to fill the gaps if they exist.

6. Be good parents

Great parents allow their children to make mistakes. They teach them all they can, and they give them wings to fly and pursue their own dreams.

In a team, we must think of ourselves as parents of each other.

And every day, if we strive to be the best we can be in what we do, we'll need to push ourselves to the limit and make a few mistakes. It's the mistakes that lead us to the truth.

US Founding Father Benjamin Franklin once wrote:

> "Perhaps the history of the errors of mankind, all things considered, is more valuable and interesting than that of their discoveries. Truth is uniform and narrow; it does not seem to require so much an active energy, as a passive aptitude of soul in order to encounter it. But error is endlessly diversified."

Fail faster. Act like a child and a parent at the same time. Be the best in the world at something every day.

How maths can help you solve people problems

In mathematics, actions like add, subtract, multiply, divide, square, etc. are known as "operations". If it isn't a number, it is probably an operation.

In business operations however, people are like the mathematical operators. People add, subtract, divide and multiply.

As any business owner will tell you, dealing with people is difficult to get right.

So, here's a tip for any managers out there. If each of your team members were an operation (+, -, x, /), which would they be?

+ ADD +
Someone who adds, adds value. They do their job well, consistently. You need to reward, motivate and nurture these important team members.

- SUBTRACT -
Someone who subtracts is not providing value. They do not do their job well (for whatever reason). You need to address this performance and attempt to turn it around. This may not be possible. If you fail to turn a subtracter into an adder, you need to remove this person from the team.

/ DIVIDE /

Someone who divides not only does their job badly but causes others to do their job badly as well. They suck up your time. They are a bad influence. They are poisonous. If you have a divider, you need to realise this quickly and remove them fast. Your team will thank you for this.

x MULTIPLY x

Someone who multiplies not only does their job well but causes others to do a better job as well. They are a catalyst for success. Success breeds success. And so if you can have more multipliers on your team, subtractors can become adders and adders can become better adders. You need to listen to and empower your multipliers. You also need to make sure they don't get bored or disillusioned. They need to believe in your vision, and they will amplify that vision for you. Look after them like the gold that they are.

So, what does your team look like?

Like this? xxx++++

Or like this? x++- -//

This simple perspective can really help when tough decisions are needed, and it can help you remember to look after your stars.

Decide what type of decision you are making before you make a decision

Your manager invites you to a meeting. Which of the following three invitations is most useful?

Meeting invite 1
We are meeting later today to discuss issue X. I need to make a decision on the issue this week because if I don't, Y will happen. I would like you all to bring all

the information you can think of that might inform how I make this decision and suggest any potential solutions. I will listen to you all and may need some time to reflect on what we will do, so a decision may or may not be reached today. It will be my decision because I will be held accountable for it, so we will not be putting it to a vote. If you have a strong view on what we should do, I want you to be totally honest about your opinion and give me reasons why, even if you think I won't agree with you..

Meeting invite 2

We are meeting later today to discuss issue X. What we choose to do on this will have long-term consequences for the business, so I'd like to make sure I understand the details. I will give my opinion if I have one, but it will be up to you to decide on the best course of action, having first fully understood all the main implications. Let's spend some time making sure we all understand the problem first, and we may need to reframe it based on what we discuss. That might be all we achieve today. If we do, that's OK, we have time.

Meeting invite 3

We're meeting later today to make a decision on issue X.

Meeting invite 3 is a very common approach. Set the meeting, set the attendees and set a topic. It's very rare to describe the expectations, as seen in 1 and 2.

The advantage of the first two approaches, of course, is that they set expectations of the attendees. They also determine how and by whom a decision is going to be made. As to which to use, see below - it depends on the type of decision.

If being this explicit in the meeting invite is not something you can see yourself doing, you can still set expectations, either in a pre-meeting email or at the start of the meeting.

It's about setting the rules of engagement. If everyone plays the game using the same rules, the game is played better.

Simply put, communicate upfront as to how the decision will be made.

How a decision is to be made is not usually discussed or made clear. Being clear can help everyone participate in a positive way.

Here are six decision types to consider:

1. Do nothing

Sometimes by doing nothing a decision gets made for you. It's not really a decision but it's what happens if you don't make one. Doing this gives up power to fate and so is not really decision making at all.

2. Democratic

This is also known as majority rule. Every person in the process has an equal say and the majority position secures the decision. Although common in government, it has two main disadvantages: i) without full support, those who didn't agree with the majority may do something unhelpful afterwards; and ii) there's a risk of creating "us versus them" groups that spill over into the culture.

3. Executive

The leader makes the decision. This type of decision making is common in business and rightly so - the leader is held accountable for the decisions being made. However, if the leader is making the decision, they have to make sure that they receive the best advice and information, making sure that their team(s) feel confident and trusted to share what's needed. If overused, executive decision making can stop more junior team members acting with courage, because they always refer to the leader to make a decision, thinking that's what is expected. Leaders can delegate their decisions and should do so where appropriate.

4. Expert

Sometimes leaders defer to the expert and ask the expert (or small group of experts) to make a decision for them. This can be appropriate where it's a specialist area of knowledge. The leader should make sure that the experts explain their decision-making process and options.

5. Consensus

This is where everyone agrees to support the decision even if they do not personally agree with it. Despite their different perspectives, all agree they can deliver the decision. It takes time though. If you have the time, this method will serve you and the team well; each person is listened to and given proper consideration. That said, it's less useful in a crisis when a more direct executive order might be needed to act quickly.

6. Unanimous

Everyone agrees. A great outcome of course but not always possible. Ask if the decision really needs to be unanimous, because if it is (or isn't), it's worth being super clear. Unanimous, of course, is very different to consensus. Because in a consensus decision, everyone agrees to follow the decision, whereas in a unanimous decision, everyone actually needs to agree with the decision itself.

If it's not clear...

Sometimes you need to discuss the issue to identify the type of decision that then needs to be made. This is an exploratory discussion leading to clarity on how the decision needs to be made. If this is the case, it may well be worth simply calling this out.

(Or just follow the process.)

Sometimes decisions can be made following a pre-agreed process. This is useful where there are predictable events that require a response. Every company has written (or unwritten) policies and procedures that simplify decision making. Sometimes the decision can just be made by following the policy. Remember to examine on a regular basis if the policy/process is fit for purpose.

Be explicit

Decision making is ultimately about having good information and making good judgements in alignment with a clear cause/purpose.

Being explicit on the type of decision being made is an important factor in making good decisions and ensuring that they are then agreed upon and carried through.

When things are going wrong, they might just be about to go right

You start your holiday with excitement and energy. Woo-hoo! No more work for two weeks, we're off!

How long does that feeling last? When do the arguments start? Unless you're off back-packing by yourself, you'll be with friends or family or both.

Here's typically what happens:

Day 1 - Excitement, chatter, interest in other people, sharing plans, news and celebrating.

Day 2 - More of the same, just a little slower but you're still all on best behaviour.

Day 3 - Starting to get tired, needing a little more space and time, starting to make less effort towards each other.

Day 4 - The arguments start. You can no longer maintain your best behaviour at all times. You start to say what you really think. Others do the same. A few disagreements maybe. Maybe a full-blown row or face-off.

Day 5 - You start to adjust to your real travelling companions, their needs and wants, your own needs and wants, and to your new environment and living space. Maybe a few apologies, a few honest and frank conversations.

Day 6 - Now you're all just being yourselves and relating to others in a truthful way, you start to find ways to enjoy yourselves together on this new level.

Day 7 - You're more relaxed and start to enjoy the holiday for what it really is.

Day 8 onwards - You're having a great time but it's time to go home.

Does that ring a bell? Have you ever been in a holiday situation like that?

The pattern repeats itself whenever a new member joins the group or there is some kind of instability such as a change in environment. You all go back a few steps until you readjust.

The pattern has a name: Form-storm-norm-perform.

- Form - The honeymoon period, everyone is on their best behaviour.
- Storm - The truth comes out, friction and strife.
- Norm - Adjusting to the reality of the group.
- Perform - Getting the best out of the group in a truthful way.

This pattern doesn't just apply to holidays. It applies to any new collaboration of two or more people.

It applies to relationships. Remember those first six months? That's the "form" period. Some people come off that six-month period wondering what happened. You're suddenly arguing about things you never used to argue about. Here's the truth - it's completely normal to have these arguments ("storm"). You need to get through them and accept the other person for who they truly are ("norm") before you can be strong as a couple ("perform").

It applies to companies. New people join a company and go through their own form-storm-norm-perform evolution before they truly settle. Some people just get out at the storm stage, but others will persist, and that's the route to performance.

It applies to projects. There's always a doom and gloom middle part of a project where the project manager feels like it's never going to happen. But it does.

It applies to sports. Setting out (form) on the path to glory (perform) requires a lot of soul searching and pain as you put the training in (storm and norm) to become the athlete you want to become.

It applies to studying. Learning a new skill is exciting at first (form), but you realise that it's very difficult to commit and put the hours in (storm) and until you manage to do that consistently (norm) you won't succeed (perform).

I've observed this pattern many, many times in life, and it's helped me enormously. When the euphoria of a new start wears off, I think "Hey, this is perfectly normal and to be expected - let's keep going" and it gives me strength.

My expectations are more realistic and I'm less prone to reacting badly when things go wrong. I had to learn this the hard way. Simon, my manager when I was at Eurocamp, said observantly, "David, you don't like it when things go wrong, do you?" He was right of course. That's still the case. I like to get things right the first time. Now I realise that that is an ideal, that the real world will hit me hard, and that I need to push through to see the success on the other side.

Give in order to receive

My grandmother taught me that the best thing about presents is the giving, not the receiving. There is great pleasure to be had in giving someone something that they truly appreciate.

To solve someone else's need or want is a great human gesture. We humans are social creatures, and the act of giving is at the heart of all great relationships.

It seems true in life that by giving we create goodwill and goodwill has value. Great relationships can exist between companies and a) their customers and b) their employees. And it all starts with giving. Giving people what they need.

For example, every time I call my bank, they answer my phone call almost straight away. When I get through, they answer my question, they are friendly and helpful. I am a very satisfied customer and, if I ever get the chance, I tell my friends what a great bank they are. I have been a loyal customer for more than 25 years and will probably be for life.

My bank attracted my attention because it solved a problem for me - it satisfied my need. In 1997, my need was that I didn't want to have to walk down the high street to the bank. It was an inconvenience. It promised 24/7 telephone banking (and later, when the time came, it provided all of this online). It made it easy for me to switch my account from my previous bank and gave me a cash reward to say thank you.

My bank provided me with what I wanted, where I wanted it, when I wanted it and how I wanted it. And it did it with a smile. I rewarded it with my business and my recommendation. It's a very positive relationship.

The positive relationship between a customer and a company has many similarities with the relationship between an employee and a company. Especially when it goes right.

If you manage people, are your team as positive about you and as loyal to you as I am to my bank?

Just as different customers have different needs and companies provide products and services to meet these needs, people at companies have needs and wants. We all do.

We need money to buy food and pay the rent. We want a purpose in life. We need to feel important and that what we do with our life matters. We want to feel in control and therefore free of unnecessary anxiety. We might want friends and need social stimulation. Maybe we want to learn, develop and grow as a person. Maybe we just want recognition and a "thank you". We want information.

Employment can provide for some of these needs. Just as great companies spend a lot of effort to understand their customers and provide what they need, I believe really great managers spend time to understand what their team truly needs and wants, and figure out how to provide it. Employees reward the company with their effort, creativity and loyalty.

(Note: people don't always know what they want. Phone manufacturers used to think that what we wanted was a smaller and smaller phone. It turns out we wanted a big flat screen. We didn't know that. True needs are often hidden, often driven by emotion not logic. Your team might say they want to be paid more. This might not be their real need. Their real need might be (say) freedom to act, recognition or purpose. It's often these deep needs that are most powerful.)

Think about the best manager you've ever worked for. Think about the best company you've ever worked for. What needs and wants did they satisfy for you? And did you give your effort in return?

When managers succeed, it's because they provide for these needs. The need could be a training opportunity. It could just be encouragement and praise. It could be a fancy job title. It could be the freedom to make decisions. It could be a company social event. It could be a clear vision of what the company is trying to achieve. It could be the sharing of useful information. When a manager or company gets this right, it seems like magic. And it requires giving first.

So many managers act as if they are the customer. In a way, that is perhaps technically correct. At least that's the way the money flows. The company pays a salary after all. I however propose that it is a fundamental error to think this way and that, although it's counterintuitive, we should start to think the other way around. Employees are customers.

If you agree with this approach, as a manager, I'd advise the following:

1. Identify what your team need and want (at both an individual level and as a group).
2. Provide it.

3. Continuously seek feedback about if you are on the right track.
4. Show appreciation.

Sometimes the best person to promote is the person who has no idea what they are doing

Here is a very common scenario in high-growth companies; you need a manager for a fast-growing team.

Do you hire in a manager for the team, or do you ask one of the most promising team members to be the manager? What if that person has never managed people before?

There are advantages to hiring externally and advantages to promoting from within.

External hire:

- Proven management skills
- Will add a fresh perspective
- *But* doesn't know the product, the people or you.

Internal hire:

- Knows the product/service intimately
- Knows the people on the team
- Knows you
- *But* doesn't have managerial experience.

There's a clear trade-off to make: product expertise with managerial inexperience versus managerial experience with product inexperience. There's no right or wrong answer to this trade-off.

Ultimately it boils down to:

- Whether you believe your internal candidate has sufficient potential
- Whether you're prepared to support them to develop their potential.

To understand their potential, I'd recommending asking:

- What is their track record to date when it comes to working relationships with others?
- How much ownership of a problem do they take?
- What positive character traits do they have and how can they take advantage of these should they manage others?
- Are they willing to take responsibility and do they want to do it?
- Will the rest of the team understand why you promoted them?
- Do you have a plan on how you can support them?

If the answers to all of the above are positive, the internal candidate is a good choice. It shows everyone else in your team that you will promote internally and there are opportunities for development.

Just be prepared to help them realise their potential.

Part 3 - question prompts

Before we move on to Part 4, here are some questions you can ask yourself to find your own growth opportunities.

> How flexible are you on moulding roles to the strengths of individuals? Do you do this too much (leaving gaps in the work to be done) or too little (missing the chance for talent to shine)?

> When you recruit, do you have a sense of urgency and treat candidates like customers?

> Do you understand the downside of your strengths? Do you understand the upside of your weaknesses?

> Do you invest in a great onboarding experience for new members of your team?

> How might you create a culture of trust to help your team open up?

> For improving performance in your team, are you usually clear if it's a capability or a competence issue that you need to address?

> Could you improve your internal communications and treat your team as equally important as your customers and investors?

> Are you clear on what type of innovation suits you best? How about your team - do you understand how they innovate best?

> Do you have an inflection point coming up where the size of your team might need a change in how you manage or organise?

> Are there instances where you could move faster if you involved fewer people or used a smaller team?

> Do you have enough slack in your system or are you always flat out with no room for contingency?

> Do you give feedback straight away? Are you clear with your feedback?

> How could you mobilise your team to provide motivation and encouragement to each other?

> Do your team take it in turns to take the load and give each other support and rest?

> Do you explain why when you ask for information, help or a task to be done? Could you do this more often?

> How might you improve how your team works together so that 1+1=3?

> Are you ruthless in removing people who hold the team back?

> Are you clear on the different types of decision and do you agree and communicate the type of decision expected on a case-by-case basis?

> Could you use the form-storm-norm-perform model to better understand team dynamics over time?

> In simple terms, how does your business help people? Can you explain it to people that way and reduce your use of jargon?

> Could you take a bet on backing the potential of up-and-coming talent on your team? How could you give them opportunities to learn?

5

Part 4: Personal growth - Being the best you can be

Chapter 1 - Know yourself

As we've seen in earlier chapters, knowing your customers and their needs is an important foundation upon which to create growth. It is the same for personal growth: knowing yourself is an important foundation if you are to grow your abilities and skills.

You may think you are an individual, but you are really not

In human stories we recognise character types known as archetypes. Much of Hollywood is built upon telling the same stories, just with different players. A typical storyline might revolve around a hero (who is also a lover or rebel) rescuing the unjustly accused and doing battle (Star Wars? Shrek?) with a malevolent magician.

Rebel, lover, magician - these are examples of archetypes. Archetypes describe unconscious patterns that drive our behaviours.

Archetypes are said to be universal; they are the shared collective unconscious that every human being has. Yet they are experienced individually and subjectively. While we all share the same archetypes, they manifest differently based on our individual consciousness and experiences. Yes, we are individuals - to a point.

We all see archetypes in each other. We all have them.

Do others see you as a hero, a visionary, a caregiver, a magician, an intellectual or a rebel?

Most of us have a blend. It turns out that I'm about 60% explorer, 20% visionary and 20% creative.

When I found this out it helped me understand how I behave. For example, a high bias towards "explorer" means that I love new places, new things and new ideas. This is useful and explains my career path in the travel sector, startups and marketing/growth. However, it also explains why I get bored easily and can tire myself out.

If you're interested in finding out your own archetypes, you can do so at this site: archetypes.com. A simple quiz leads you to your personal blend.

Knowing your archetypes is a shortcut to understanding your strengths. Knowing your strengths is a shortcut to understanding your weaknesses.

Your strengths are your weaknesses

My grandmother once told me a story about how my younger self was prone to impulsive urges.

We were walking past a shop and in the window was a toy car. I really wanted that toy car and started pleading with my grandma to buy it.

She asked me how much pocket money I had, and whatever I had was not enough. She said that we could come back at the weekend when I would have received some pocket money and had a chance to save up for it.

I was not happy. I did not want to wait until the weekend. I can't imagine it was a pleasant scene. Still, my grandma (rightly so) stood firm and we did not buy the car. Not then and not at the weekend, because by then I was no longer interested in the car.

She told me this story about my younger self when I was a teenager. She said she was worried about my impulsive nature. It's true, I do have an impulsive nature. And I love it. I've learnt to control spending urges, but there have been many times in life when this side of my character has served me well. I've done many unusual things in life that have left a richness of experience, and that in part is due to my willingness to make instant decisions and "do".

Impulsiveness can be a weakness; it can also be a strength. The same is true I find of most personality traits. It all depends on context. Most traits have a use. So if you can understand better who you are and put yourself into situations that suit your personality, you'll find a good path.

Very persuasive, tenacious and curious? Great if you are an investigative journalist or salesperson. Not very good at writing? Perhaps sales works better for you than journalism.

I don't believe that we have strengths or weaknesses. I believe instead that we all have certain personality traits that are amplified, that we use and abuse, and that in the right context can be strengths.

There are no strengths and weaknesses, only context.

The dark side can lead to unnatural abilities

In the 1977 movie *Star Wars*, the sage-like character Obi-Wan Kenobi planted the following phrase into our collective consciousness:

> "Use the force, Luke."

This scene was towards the end of the original *Star Wars* movie in a touch-and-go moment where Luke (the unlikely hero) was flying his X-wing fighter in close to try and bomb and destroy the evil Empire's Death Star spaceship.

My understanding is that the force is a metaphor for the spiritual power of humanity that can be harnessed for good purpose. There is, of course, the dark side to the force as well - as harnessed by the enemy, Darth Vader.

All of us - it seems - have a dark side. Hopefully, your dark side doesn't cause you to create a universe-dominating autocracy. Still, it's there. The dark side is the part of your character that you don't really like that much. It is the part of you that you feel embarrassed about. It's your Achilles heel. It's there when you can't really be your best self. It's there when you sabotage yourself. Some psychologists have called this the "shadow self".

You may think it's a good idea to keep your dark side under wraps. Keep it under control. I used to think that too. I've recently discovered that there is some real latent (untapped) growth potential to be had by exploring this dark side. That may sound like a contradiction, but it's not. It is, however, uncomfortable and takes some time to work through. You may need a coach to help you through it.

With my coach (who, as coincidence would have it, is also called Luke), I started out by writing down all the things I could think of that I do well and all the behaviours that I'm proud of. Luke then challenged me to write down a list of the things I was less proud of, that trip me up or that I might regret.

This territory is dark stuff. It takes time to admit it and write it down.

(By the way, as it happens, the origin of the word Luke is "light-giving", derived from the Greek name Louka. How apt!)

I'll share one example. I have a tendency to be slightly hyperactive. I will go go go go go all day long, sometimes all week long, sometimes for a few weeks. I am incredibly productive during this time. I don't really rest. I might just grab a cup of tea before cracking on again. I probably don't take enough lunch breaks. It's not quite manic, but it's in that direction. All this activity, this action, can be very powerful (if applied to meaningful things to solve or do). It means I can get a lot done in a very short space of time. Action-orientated, I can smash things through and get stuff done. It is a strength if you look at it that way but, as I said before, strengths are weaknesses. The downside is that when you do that to yourself, eventually your body says no thank you. And for me, it can take quite some time before I get to that point. I can run on adrenaline for weeks and then there comes a point where I absolutely just hit a wall and I'm useless. I'm useless for as many days as it takes me to get my energy back and get some balance in my life - so this strength has a downside.

In the past I've tried to moderate this behaviour by saying things like "It's a marathon, not a sprint." This simple phrase clearly didn't hit the mark, because I kept doing it and finding myself burnt out. It's my duty to turn up at work ready to do my best, and being burnt out isn't that.

What is needed is an affirmation that balances out the shadow behaviour.

With Luke, he suggested that we work on a phrase starting with "It's like me to…".

It took a while but we ended up with this:

> "It's like me to be as intense with my recovery as I am with my action".

This is an affirmation. It is something that I want to do, that I can do. It doesn't prevent me from having intense action. It does however give me a way to recover from my intense action by practising intense recovery. Now when I say this to myself, I see value in the act of recovery. Just as an athlete needs to recover from a difficult workout to make that workout count, I also need to recover from intense creative work, physical effort or mental effort. Being more of an introvert, I need "time out" after a period of social activity before I can enjoy a fresh bout.

"It's like me to..." is quite a powerful phrase. It gives me permission to strive towards certain qualities or goals rather than feel like a failure if I don't exhibit or achieve them. ("I always" by comparison would lead to more guilt and a feeling of falling short.)

An affirmation works well if it's short, catchy and easy to remember. It's inspirational. You won't always achieve your stated goal, but you'll be happy to strive towards it.

So, don't be afraid to visit your shadow. There is a powerful force there to use if you let yourself. It can be a powerful driver of growth.

There's no I in team but there is a me

Many people, in my opinion, are often not true to themselves. They follow other people's rules, wear clothes to fit in with what other people think or say things to create an image of themselves that they want to portray to others. It's pretty rare to just be yourself, especially at work.

As soon as you are yourself, your real self, you have a feeling. I'm not sure I can describe it, but I know it when I feel it.

And when some people in a group start being themselves, others do the same. It's contagious and in a good way. Sometimes it can create tension, but at least that tension is transparent, not hidden away. Issues and problems when out in the open are no longer problems - they are opportunities to do something right, to make something happen.

The best-performing teams I've led are those in which I could be myself. I'm generally a responsible person, but I too have a rebellious side which comes out to play every now and again. In those teams, my maverick nature was not hidden. Equally, my frustration - when I wasn't happy with the quality of work performed - wasn't hidden either. We did good together. We rocked.

As the band Primal Scream once noted:

> "Together we got power, apart we got pow-wow."

When each person can be free to be themselves and express themselves through their work, they come home at the end of the day knowing they did something meaningful and look forward to waking up and doing more.

High-performing teams are honest teams. The first step to an honest team is people being themselves. Leaders can take the initiative and be themselves first. It takes courage but it feels good. And paradoxically, it's the path to success.

Go live. Be yourself. Feel good and enjoy the ride.

The best version of you is the "warts and all" version

Being yourself is all very well, but what is that? What does it mean to be authentic?

I work with marketing teams. In marketing it's important, if you sell through a brand, to define that brand. What does it stand for? What does it promise? What is its tone of voice? Does it stand for value, choice, expertise or being low cost? Is it maverick, conservative, fun or serious? And so on.

By doing this work, marketing teams define the brand essence and then work to ensure their products, service, culture and reputation capture it.

I thought - if you can do that for a brand, can you do it for an individual?

If I could write down what it means to be me at work, it would finesse my thinking and it would give me something to align to. If I wrote it down, I could focus on being that best self and bringing it to work. I could understand my purpose, my values, my tone of voice and so on. Just as you come to know what to expect from a brand, people could come to know what to expect from me. I shared it with my peers and my direct reports. They appreciated me being vulnerable and open. And as a result, I felt I could be myself, more often - leading to better motivation and, therefore, better confidence and results.

It turned out to be a very useful exercise and I'll share the output here.

Much of it is based on the following list of questions I asked myself. You could use these as a prompt for questions to ask yourself. My answers include some honest admission of my flaws. My best version of me is a "warts and all" version. To be useful, it needs to be truthful.

DNA: David Norris, Authentic. Being the best version of me - A guide. How to get the best from me. What I can offer. How I like to work.

What do you do?

- I'm a manager, exec, mentor and community leader.

Who do you serve?

- My family
- Holiday Extras customers
- ExecCo colleagues
- Holiday Extras Group Board
- Holiday Extras wider leadership team
- Marketing and trading teams
- The local skateboarding community
- Business founders who I advise.

What are your strengths?

- Seeing patterns and the big picture, simplifying things, being a reductionist, an essentialist
- Explaining the big picture, communicating key points, summarising key issues and clarifying details
- Empathy, seeing the other person's point of view
- Finding common ground, being diplomatic
- Patience and calmness
- Openness to new ideas
- Following through and taking responsibility
- Nurturing others and building teams
- Critical thinking
- Problem solving
- Online trading, online business models.

What do you enjoy doing?

- Coaching (helping others to be the best they can be)
- Advising and mentoring (reacting to specific topics)
- Exploring new concepts, ideas or methods
- Creative thinking
- Problem solving
- Exploring
- Travelling
- Being outdoors
- Action sports and exercise (esp. skiing, cycling, climbing and skateboarding)
- Learning from stories (biography, history, novels and movies).

What are your values and character?

- Be pioneering: Adventurous, pioneering, curious.
- Be open minded: Open, objective, wise.
- Be kind: Empathetic, considerate, caring.
- Be real: Clear, simple, concise, authentic.
- Be independent: Resourceful, self-sufficient.

What makes your life worth living?

- Seeing my children develop and grow
- Enjoying good times together with my wife
- Helping people to realise their potential
- Helping achieve a business growth mission
- Learning about new ideas and concepts
- Coaching and advising others
- Exploring the world, experiencing different cultures and places
- Experiencing the beauty of nature
- Exercising and staying fit

- Spending time with friends and family, good conversation
- Developing the local skateboarding community
- Feeling a sense of accomplishment from skateboarding, skiing and other action sports.

What is your purpose?

- Providing leadership and mentoring leaders to help people succeed with growth-generating enterprises or experiences (such as travel, sport and new business ventures).

What does that mean?

- Leadership: Setting direction and context, making decisions if needed, providing advice.
- Mentoring: Asking the right questions, helping frame challenges, agreeing priorities, providing help and assistance.
- Growth generation: I have a particular interest in what are the levers for growth, not just keeping the status quo.
- Enterprises: New ventures, businesses, projects or initiatives.
- Experiences: Personal growth through adventure, learning, challenges.

What's your purpose in two words?

- Adventurous growth.

What do you need to be at your best?

- Workspace: office environment, dual monitors, high desk.
- 30 minutes of quiet at lunch to reflect and take stock.
- I do my best desk work in the morning, first thing. I like to keep that time free to get ready for the day, clear messages and get organised.
- If I am presenting or chairing a meeting, I need plenty of time in advance

to prepare.
- I prefer to discuss issues face to face rather than over text/email.
- Time to reflect and recharge after social interactions.
- Daily exercise (early in the day) and early bedtime to maintain my energy.
- Regular food and drink, otherwise I can lose focus.
- Collaborate on projects rather than working alone.

What is your working style?

- I have an experimental nature. I iterate with the resources at hand rather than visioning.
- I like to create a framework/structure and build on it if needed. Bullet points first, then add detail afterwards.
- I am a reductionist. I look at a topic and try to figure out the root causes or key issues.
- I delegate. I like to give people freedom to thrive, and I coach them rather than direct them.
- I edit better than I draft. Give me content and I can finesse it.

How can I get the best out of you?

- When opening a meeting, set the context and goal of the meeting.
- When wishing to discuss an issue, find time to talk with me rather than trying to do it over email or messages.
- Give me plenty of lead time if you need my input or help.
- Explain why you are trying to solve a problem, not just present the problem.
- Solve a problem/run a project together.
- Remind me if I failed to follow up on something. I will be grateful for the nudge.

What do you need help with?

- I find it difficult to participate in a meeting and simultaneously take notes. I need a note-taker.
- Initiating meetings or setting up project working groups. I welcome someone to book the follow-ups for me.
- Being reminded of who needs to know what following a decision/discussion. I'm not a natural broadcaster and so I don't always amplify outwards as much as I could.

So - go on - see if you can create your own guide. Use this framework if it's helpful. It was this process that led me to pulling this book together. My purpose is adventurous growth - this book helps to serve that purpose.

Chapter 2 - Stay in control

One of the challenges of working in a growth-focussed environment is staying organised and knowing where to apply your energy. In this section, I reflect on approaches that have helped me stay in control and keep my head above water.

To do more things, do fewer things

Having a lot on your plate at work can be challenging. Challenging busy is good. Stressful busy is not good.

When someone tells me they're really busy, I sometimes quip, "It's called job security." Which is unfair and probably untrue, so I should probably stop doing that.

Just like everyone else, there are days when I feel the pressure.

I have a tried-and-tested tactic to deal with the pressure. I simply ask myself one question:

If you did just three things today, what would they be?

It's an excellent way to cut to the heart of what matters most.

It turns out that you can really get through a lot of effective work if you limit yourself to only focussing on a few important things at a time.

If you don't run your inbox, it will run you

Like most of you, I get a lot of email. I rarely however have an overflowing inbox. How is that possible? It's not easy, that's for sure.

I try to keep the number of emails that I still need to deal with at below 20. That's simply because if they go onto more than two pages it gets noisy. One page or less and it feels like I'm in control of my inbox and my inbox is not in control of me.

I like to hit "inbox zero" a few times a week if I can. Most of the time I'm happy if there's fewer than 20 things in the inbox.

Here are seven techniques I use:
   (Note: I use Google Apps, so these tips will make sense to you if you also use Google for mail. If not, some of the principles will still apply.)

1. Unsubscribe

Sounds obvious. It's all about reducing unnecessary distractions. If I ever find myself on an email list I don't want to be on, I unsubscribe immediately there and then. This also extends to some of the notification messages I get from LinkedIn, Twitter, Slack, etc. Not all notifications are useful, so I cull the least useful and save my attention for the ones I want to actually receive. A small amount of configuration pays off in the long term.

2. Filter newsletters out of the inbox

For the subscriptions I do have, I filter these out of my inbox to a separate folder.

Here's how the filter looks in Gmail.

- Matches: from:(address@domain.com)
- Do this: Skip Inbox, Apply label "Alerts".

They remain unread but they're not in my inbox. When I check my email on my phone away from my desk, I only want to see what's important. Leaving the newsletters and alerts for when I'm back at my desk helps me to process important stuff quickly when I'm on the move.

3. Flag as follow-up/starred

My email system is based around the concept that an email is in one of three states: unread, read or flagged.

On reading an email I do one of four things:

- Action - Read and reply straight away.
- Action - Read, no follow up needed.
- Defer action - Read but flag to follow up later (it might require research, further thought or more time to answer than I have at the time).
- No action - See the headline and know that I do not need to read it. So just mark as read without having read it.

I follow these four rules whether I'm on my phone or laptop.

This means that I only have in my inbox things that need action or need reading.

4. Delay delivery - scheduled send

People often deal with their inbox from the most recent message first. This makes sense, especially on a thread as the most recent email will contain the most up-to-date information.

Sometimes I know that the time I might be hitting send may not be the optimal time to grab someone's attention. I might be sending an email at 6pm on a Friday night. In that situation, as long as it's not super urgent, it is worth sending the email but delaying the arrival until 9.30am Monday. This way you'll be at the top of their to-do list and not the bottom. (It also means you won't get a reply over the weekend.)

5. Email myself

If I think of something I need to do or chase up, I will email myself. This works quite well if, for example, I think of something at the weekend. It means that my future self is reminded of the action on Monday morning.

6. Send fewer emails

The more email you send, the more you receive. Email does not equal work or results. Often, it's more effective to go talk to someone face to face or call them up. Save email for transmitting or requesting information. It's not a great medium for a conversation.

7. Never leave phone by my bed

One key ingredient of being in control of email is that you can relax and switch off when you need to. I check my email at all sorts of times of day, but I never leave my phone by my bed. I don't want email to be the first thing or last thing I do each day. I noticed that simply leaving the phone to charge downstairs in the kitchen allows me to switch off before bedtime and ease into the day and wake up before getting online.

You can be more creative by changing your creative space and time

Clustering meetings in your calendar can boost creativity and output.

A third to half of my week is booked up before the week starts, in meetings. Sometimes more than half.

Some people like to have some slack around their meetings so they have time to prepare or follow up after each. I find that to be less productive. Here's why.

Having half an hour here and half an hour there of free time doesn't allow for doing anything of substance. Half an hour is useful for firing off a few emails, making a phone call or clearing your inbox - but that's about it.

Unblock creativity with smart scheduling

If I have a two- to three-hour block at my desk, I can start to think about doing something constructive - and it's these constructive, proactive tasks that make a difference in the long term.

When scheduling my calendar, I prefer to block meetings into two- to three-hour windows, leaving the rest of the day for desk work. That way I can focus, concentrate and produce something of long-term value. If you switch away from a thinking task whilst halfway through, it'll end up taking you twice as long.

Equally, if I am doing quickfire reactive tasks (such as inbox clearance), I'll do those tasks together in short bursts.

You can shape creativity by shaping the environment in which you create. A key part of that environment is your schedule.

You don't manage time, you make it

Consider these two statements:

- I'll make time to do it.
- I'll find time to do it.

If you ask someone to do something, which response do you think is more convincing? "I'll make time", right?

When someone says they'll make time to do something, you know they will. It means that it will go to the top of their to-do list - it will be top priority.

When someone says they'll find time, it sounds like they'll do what they already had planned, and they hope to find a gap where they might fit it in.

You know something is important when you make time for it. Look at your own week. What do you make time for?

Do you make time for...

- having a one-to-one with your team members?
- doing some exercise?
- putting your kids to bed?
- writing an article?
- hitting your reporting deadlines?
- spending time to give good feedback to candidates who applied to work at your company?
- listening to your customers?
- eating healthily?

- talking with your partner?
- sleeping?
- updating team members on the progress of a project?
- building relationships in your industry?
- learning?
- clearing your inbox?

Some of the above may or may not apply to you. I'm not saying you should or shouldn't do any of these things. I'm pointing out that if you think carefully about what you make time to do versus what you find time to do, it will be like looking in the mirror. A time management mirror. A prioritisation mirror.

Once you've seen what's in the mirror, you can reflect(!) and decide if you really are making time for the most important things.

Language has a way of revealing truths in our behaviour. The phrase "I'll make time" reveals a lot that we can learn from.

Chapter 3 - Be your best

I like to leave work every day and be able to say that today I did what I do best. I also want my team to be able to say the same thing. Pushing yourself to be the best you can be doesn't mean comparing yourself to other people. The only person you are competing with is yourself.

You're not going to fluke success

Rugby World Cup-winning former England fly-half Jonny Wilkinson retired from the sport at the end of the 2013-14 season.

I remember sitting on the edge of my seat watching the 2003 Rugby World Cup Final against Australia. England won thanks to a drop kick by Wilkinson just 26 seconds before the end of the match. He became a national hero.

Former All Blacks player Dan Carter is one of the best fly-halfs in the world. He says he learned a lot from Wilkinson:

> "What Jonny Wilkinson has taught me most is that you're not going to fluke success."

Wilkinson was one of the hardest working men in rugby. He trained longer and harder than anyone else. His famous kick was practised day in day out year after year after year. Sure he had talent, sure he had ability. What set him apart was hard work.

This determination and application could be seen from an early age. His old schoolmaster Steve Bates said of him:

> "Jonny had an awful lot of determination and dedication, he liked to do things properly. It was all pretty exceptional for a schoolboy in those days."

There's a lesson there for all of us. Nothing comes easy in life. Hard work is hard. It's called work for a reason. It requires mental strength to keep going when others give up.

Determination, grit, application - whatever you call it, it's not a fluke. It's entirely within our control.

I remember something my mum said when I'd had a tough day. She said, "Well, it's called work for a reason!" Sometimes work can be fun and sometimes it's, well, just hard work.

Behind the big success stories, behind the big exits, behind the startups that become household names - behind all of this, there's an awful lot of hard work.

100% is easier than 98%

Olympic gold medal-winning cyclist Chris Hoy knew what commitment was. To develop his power, he'd train on a stationary bike, so hard that it hurt.

In 2012, the Daily Mail newspaper quoted him as saying:

> "It's the worst pain imaginable... You feel as if you are dying. You're physically sick and you writhe around on a mat in a world of pain until you can form a foetal position, which you stay in for 15 minutes thinking you can't go on."

This is hard. This is commitment. It was all or nothing.

And nothing is so close to everything...

Having an option to quit and not do something means you might quit and not do something. Not giving yourself that option means you won't.

Nic Brisbourne, Managing Partner at venture capital (VC) firm Forward Partners (and my former manager and business partner), said to me:

> "100% commitment is easier than 98%."

Nic blogged every workday for years. He had a crazy workload and yet he still made time to blog. When we talked about it, he explained that committing 100% is easier than 98%. The 2% difference is the chance you give yourself to opt out.

If we fail to meet our commitments, it's because we either take on too many commitments or because we give ourselves the option of 98% being good enough. 98% becomes 96% becomes 90%, and soon we haven't come close to what we wanted to achieve.

I learned from Nic to commit carefully but to commit fully.

The most talented are not the most successful

In 2012, the Independent newspaper quoted Dave Brailsford, Principal of Team Sky, as saying:

> "You have to work out, is this athlete intrinsically driven? Is there that burning desire inside them, to continue to compete, to continue to improve, to continue to go through all the pain and the hard work, the nutrition, the lifestyle, the sacrifices you have to make? If you look at all the great champions... it's not to do with anyone outside, it's what's inside them, they're special in that respect. And if you haven't got that, it doesn't matter how much talent you've got, you're never going to get sustained success."

The Tour de France is one of the most demanding sporting competitions in the world. Its champions have to work their socks off for months to be in top condition for this gruelling three-week cycle race. They have the drive to dedicate themselves to the training required. When it comes down to the critical moments in the race, they will be prepared to suffer - really suffer to beat their rivals. You cannot win this event without going through an awful lot of pain and sacrifice. It requires not only physical endurance but mental and emotional endurance too. Yes, talent is needed, but without drive, it comes to nothing.

Dave Brailsford's observation on drive could equally apply to business leaders. There are highs and lows, winning days and losing days. It takes a driven team to succeed.

When I look back at the successful entrepreneurs I know, have met or have worked for, one thing they share is drive. This drive and passion sustains their vision, feeds their team and inspires their investors.

To be the boss, act like the boss

I remember early in my career a conversation I had with our CEO, Steve. He said, "David, if you want to be the boss, act like the boss."

I can't recall exactly what we were talking about but I remember the quote. At that stage in my career I was a middle manager. I wasn't on the leadership team. I wasn't setting company direction or strategy. I would seek approval for decisions. I would complete projects and tasks to the best of my ability.

Steve was encouraging me to develop my leadership skills and he used the phrase "to be the boss, act like the boss" as a way to explain to me that people are promoted for displaying the behaviours needed in the more senior role. He didn't mean to be bossy. Far from it. For me, it would mean forming my own opinions, suggesting, directing and showing initiative. It would mean acting in an assertive way, demonstrating positive behaviours and acting on feedback.

Good leaders are role models and we can learn a lot by emulating them. However, this does come with an unwanted side effect: business-speak. I've noticed that in their effort to progress, some mid-level managers in companies use abstract business jargon and language that you just wouldn't use in everyday life more than they need to. By contrast, all the CEOs I have had the chance to work with are straight talking and don't need to polish their language with complex jargon.

So, to act like the boss and do it well means focussing on the key issues and talking straight. Avoid jargon. Speak and write to connect to the widest possible audience. Doing this creates opportunity, because you are displaying behaviours that are truly valued. Abstractions and jargon may sound clever but they only serve to confuse.

Being the boss is many things. It means acting in the best interests of the company and its customers at all times. It also means being your version of the boss, being the authentic you and not copying other leaders. Great leaders are authentic, unique and vulnerable, not copycats.

Go fast alone or further together

Networking or notworking?

I sometime joke that I'm off to a notworking event. When I have a lot to do, networking can seem like a complete waste of time as it doesn't help me tick things off my to-do list. I'm not a natural networker. I'm more introvert than extrovert. In fact, I've had to learn how to do networking and I'll share some tips on that in a moment.

Paradoxically, I've found some of the most valuable moments in my career to be moments that I thought least valuable at the time.

I count myself lucky that I have a large network of people I know in the travel and tech space. It's an accumulation of all the company events I've been to, networking events I've attended, LinkedIn connections I've made and relationships I've made through work over the years. Very few of those events seemed important at the time but this network is like a bank account that pays compound interest. Those contacts move on from company to company. The capable ones are promoted and end up in useful positions of influence. As a senior leader in my company, it's my job to stay in touch with the outside world and stay abreast of trends and ideas. I also can connect people inside and outside the company. This all has value, and it is an accumulated value that I've nurtured over time.

Why is it important? For any new initiative, I am venturing into the unknown. If there are people who have been there before, I can ask for advice and support. Equally, I'm a big believer of "paying it forward" and looking for opportunities to help others. Sometimes these favours pay back, sometimes they don't, but they rarely cost a lot of effort. And they are worthwhile in their own right, because I am helping others on their own growth journey.

I am a member of a group coaching network, the COO Roundtable, through which I meet my peers on a monthly basis to share issues and problems we are working on. I attend industry conferences put on by partners such as Salesforce and Google. At these events I meet fellow executives. I sometimes attend conferences around a specific topic (e.g. this year I was at the AI Summit at London Tech Week). I mentor a startup founder once a month (during which I always learn something, even if I am the one being the mentor). I am involved in a local charity as a director, and I am a committee member of a couple of community groups.

If I'm stuck, rather than struggle on alone (such is my character), I've learned to ask myself who I know who could help. This is probably the single most important lesson learned in my personal growth journey. Who I know is often a result of networking. And the payback from networking is not immediate - it is measured in years and decades.

If you're not a natural networker/notworker(!), here are a few tips:

1. Do your homework. Try and find the attendee list. Find something out about the companies or people attending. Look at their public social feeds - this can be great for more personal icebreakers.
2. Arrive early. In an empty room it's much more natural to strike up conversations with other early arrivals. You'll also have more time to relax and get into the zone.
3. Ask questions. At the end of a talk, stick your hand up, introduce yourself and your company and ask a question. It means everyone in

the room now knows who you are and, if they are interested, they may come talk to you in the break.

4. Go up to someone who asked a question. "That was a great point you made at the end there. Hi, I'm David."

5. If someone is alone, just walk up to them and say hello. They probably feel as awkward as you do. Ask a simple, opening question that gets them talking about themselves. "What did you make of that talk?" "Did you have to come far today?" Find something you have in common.

6. Look at people's feet in a group. If they are pointing at each other, they are deeply engaged in a conversation and you shouldn't break their flow. If they are pointing outwards to the room, they are open to having someone join in.

7. If there is food or drink and there are tables (e.g. standing tables) a simple, "Do you mind if I join you?" can be enough to join in.

8. Practise explaining who you are and your role if you are asked. Give them something to respond to so that there's a hook for a follow-on conversation. "Hi! I'm David, I'm Chief Growth Officer at Holiday Extras. That means I focus on strategy and marketing although I was a VC previously and have worked in a few startups. We're based in Kent, and I live with my wife in Deal with four teenagers and a dog. How about you? Where do you live?" By doing this, I'm not telling my life story, but I've provided seven or eight different things that someone might be interested in. Kent, teenagers, marketing, startups, dogs, etc. You'll be unlucky if there is no follow-on and the conversation should develop naturally.

9. Work the room. Don't spend the whole session with one person. It's natural and expected that you can break off.

10. Introduce people. If you can, introduce someone you are speaking with to another new person, and explain to the newcomer what you are talking about. This makes them feel welcome and included.

11. Take time out. Sometimes as an introvert I need to calm my head. I go to the bathroom and take five, reenergise and come back.

12. Listen. A great listener is always welcome. Ask follow-on questions

and show curiosity.

I can't say I look forward to networking but I've had practice and so I can do it. Like anything, you suck at it unless you practise.

Networking is not notworking. It just has a longer payback period. It's one of those important but non-urgent things. It's rarely a waste of time if you think of it as an investment in your relationships and knowledge.

Grow your network by growing other people's networks

Your odds for achieving entrepreneurial success are improved by getting introduced to potential customers, investors, candidates, analysts and partners.

However, there's a right way and a wrong way to ask for and make introductions. As I often find myself in the position of making introductions, I've found a method that I'd encourage others to use. (If you are someone looking for introductions, take note.)

The "double-opt-in" method of making introductions

An introduction involves three people.
   Person 1 - wants to be introduced to person 3
   Person 2 - knows person 2 and person 3
   Person 3 - knows person 2

I am often in the position of person 2. Person 1 emails me asking that I introduce them to person 3.

For me to want to do this, I need to feel that:

1. I rate person 1 enough to make the introduction (they are known to me

and I trust them).

2. I believe the introduction will be of use to person 3 (therefore, I need to understand the reason for the introduction).

I also need a way to say no if it's not relevant to me.

If you're asking me to make an introduction, make sure you:

- Remind me how we know each other/when we spoke (if relevant).
- Explain what you need help with.
- Explain who you would like to be put in contact with.
- Ask if I know the person well enough to make the introduction.
- Give me an out so I can decline politely if I need to.
- Do this with me directly, not via LinkedIn.

I will then approach the person, asking if they'd like to be introduced and giving some background information. If your email is good, I will just need to copy/paste some key lines and not have to think too hard about drafting my own copy.

I'm asking the person if they are willing to accept the introduction. I have opt-in from you (person 1). Now I need opt-in from person 3. If person 3 responds with a yes, I make the introduction. It's now a double-opt-in. Both parties want the introduction to go ahead.

This sounds like a lot of effort and you might just want to skip the whole thing or just quickly fire off an email, cc-ing both parties. This is faster and optimises for your time but it doesn't optimise for impact. If you do an introduction well, it stands you in good stead, because you will be seen as adding value by both parties and you will have increased your relationship equity. Relationships are made and destroyed one conversation at a time. Relationships are like bank accounts: you can save and expand your account or you can deplete it. An introduction can do both, depending on whether it's done well or badly. You can grow the strength of your network by helping others to grow theirs.

With that in mind, my actual introduction email might be something like this:

Subject: Elizabeth < > Joe

Dear Elizabeth and Joe,

As promised, an introduction.

Elizabeth: As I explained, Joe and I used to work together at [company name]. He's got a knack for building amazing products and he's just started a new venture and is looking for advice on [subject]. Given your experience, I thought you'd be a great person for him to learn from.

Joe: Elizabeth is [job title] at [company name] and she is probably the smartest person I know when it comes to [topic].

I'm sure you'd both have a lot of mutual interest to discuss so I'll leave you to connect directly.

All the best,
  David

Now it's over to you to honour the deal.

- Respond quickly and politely. Cc me so I know you have connected but move me to bcc so I don't stay in the thread.
- Come back to me once you've met to let me know how you get on.

You'd be amazed how many people don't think about introductions like this.

Principles at work

- Provide enough information.
- Offer a way out.
- Make it easy.
- Respect the reputations of all parties.
- Follow up and say thank you.

Investing in other people is an investment in yourself.

To progress, make yourself redundant

Let's continue on the theme of personal progression. There's a paradox I discovered early in my career, which is that in order to progress in an organisation and achieve promotion, the most important thing you can do is focus on the progression of your team, not yourself.

Imagine an opportunity arises for promotion. If you are interested in this opportunity and you already have responsibilities within the company, the question will arise as to who will do your current job if you take on the new role. If you've done a good job of developing your team, they will be able to take up where you leave off and they will have the skills and talent to replace you.

Some people hold onto their expertise and knowledge. They see it as being their personal currency - something that gives them value and makes them needed by their organisation. In extreme cases, these individuals are known as being a single point of failure. If they were to leave, it would leave the company in the lurch. They don't share their knowledge and skills. However, what happens when opportunities for progression arise is they are passed over because the company can't afford to take them out of their current role.

To give yourself the best chance of progression, develop your team so that they can do more and more of your job. Helping others is the best way to help yourself.

Not working can make you more effective

Where do you get your ideas?

I get my best ones in all sorts of strange places - in the shower, walking for the bus, on my bike. Rarely do ideas come to me at my desk.

Archimedes had his "Eureka" moment in the bath. You might do too.

CEOs seem to have ideas at the weekend. That's no coincidence.

Creativity is an elusive thing. Try too hard and you'll not get anywhere. Ideas seem to have a life of their own and they are definitely not 9 to 5 office workers.

Here's something I learnt about ideas that really has helped me find more of these little creatures.

If I think about a problem hard and consciously try to start solving it, it plants a seed in my brain. But unless I've solved this problem before, rarely will a new idea form from conscious thought.

It's the unconscious mind which unlocks ideas. How scientifically true this is I cannot say. From experience though, I can say for sure that your unconscious mind continues to work on a problem long after your conscious mind has switched off.

You can be daydreaming in the shower and then pow! It comes to you. Taking that idea back into the conscious world, you can do something with it and get cracking.

If you are short of ideas, discuss the issue at hand with someone and then leave it for a day or two. The unconscious mind will work it over and you might come up with new ways of looking at the situation.

Getting started is often the most important thing you can do. Just start the thinking process consciously. Then pause. Reflect (not consciously). Wait. Discuss again. Reflect.

To really tune into a problem, you sometimes need to tune out.

Part 4 - question prompts

Before we wrap up, here are some questions you can ask yourself to find your own growth opportunities.

> What kind of archetypes represent you?

> Do you understand your personality traits and how they translate into potential strengths (and therefore weaknesses)? Are there more opportunities to use your strengths or find ways to manage your weaknesses?

> Could you face into fear more? Would it help you if you knew that behind the fear is where your greatest treasures lie?

> Do you bring your real self to work or do you hide behind a false persona?

> Are you clear on what makes you you? Could you write it down and share it with others?

> Could you start every day by quickly checking in with yourself and taking note of the top three tasks on your to-do list?

> Do you send more email than you need to? Who runs your inbox, you or

your email?

> Could you be more effective by tweaking the space in which you work?

> Do you make time for what matters most?

> Are you prepared to put in the effort to do something well? Are you prepared to commit 100%?

> Do you fall into the trap of thinking that successful people must be more talented than you? Or are you prepared to draw strength from the fact that success is mostly down to resilience and hard work?

> How could you act more like the person you want to become?

> Are you holding onto work that you could delegate or train others to do? Is this holding you back?

> Could you invest more in making connections and getting out of the office more? Do you help others to connect?

6

The Beginning

When does a day start? When does it end?

I know when it's light outside because I can see inside the house without putting the lights on. I know when it's nighttime because there are no shadows from the sun, and I need a torch to find my way.

However, there is no single moment when night becomes day. It doesn't suddenly become light from dark or dark from light. As the world turns on its axis, the sun sets over a period of minutes or hours. At sunset it is still light.

Most things that our language defines as opposites are not in fact opposites. Day and night are not opposites. They are the same thing. It is always day and it's always night. It just depends on where you are standing.

I've found this to be the case with many things in life. Work and play. Energy and rest. Action and reflection. Strengths and weaknesses. Growth and decay.

When you look at two opposites, you may find it difficult to identify the precise point at which one becomes the other. When does non-urgent become urgent? When does dirty become clean? There are degrees of urgency and there are degrees of cleanliness.

As soon as you start seeing this pattern, it's difficult to unsee it. But seeing helps us find opportunities for growth in what might otherwise be contradictions.

So, this is not the end of the book. It's not the end because it doesn't really have a beginning. It's definitely not finished, because as soon as I publish I will want to edit and add to it. I will no doubt become embarrassed to see how my younger self was so naive. It will become out of date.

But if it's helped just one reader in any small way on their own journey of growth, whether that be in business or on a personal level, I will be happy.

Thank you for reading and good luck embracing the paradox of growth.

Remember, the only thing you can rely on is gravity!

David

7

Recommended reading

Here are a few selected books that have helped me on my way and that I would recommend to further develop your thinking and approach.

Finding growth

The Black Swan: The Impact of the Highly Improbable - Nassim Nicholas Taleb

We all deal with risk on a daily basis, whether we recognise it or not. This is a thought-provoking discussion on uncertainty and probability. Our world does not operate as we like to predict it will; every so often there are "Black Swan" events that are so unlikely to happen but do.

The Origin of Wealth: Evolution, Complexity, and the Radical Remaking of Economics - Eric Beinhocker

Of all of the books on this list, this one gave me the biggest step change in my thinking. It explores an alternative view of economics - one that is more aligned with quantum physics, evolutionary theory and behavioural psychology than classical economics. It sounds heavy but it's not; it's a really interesting exploration of how emergent systems work. In short, if you want to understand why our society is the way it is, you'll find this book fascinating.

Sapiens: A Brief History of Humankind - Yuval Noah Harari

If there is one book to read on this entire list, this is it. To understand how humans act, to understand our history and our destiny, this is the most profoundly well-written book I have ever read. Can't really say more than that.

The Mom Test - Rob Fitzpatrick

If you ask your mum whether your idea is a good one, you have two problems. Firstly, she is not your customer. Secondly, she won't want to hurt your feelings. Rob's excellent book explains how to talk to customers and really learn if your business idea is actually a good one when everyone around you tells you it is. Very practical and straightforward, this is a must read for startup founders.

Talking to Humans - Giff Constable

Conducting interviews with customers without loading them with your own bias is a skill worth learning. This very simple, practical book gives you some excellent tips on how to do it well.

Unlocking growth

Influence - Robert B. Cialdini

The tricks of the trade. What techniques are used by folks to influence each other, why do they work, and how can you "protect yourself" from these techniques? Equally as useful if you are selling or if you are being sold to. Fascinating.

Why we Buy - Paco Underhill

This guy has spent decades observing consumer behaviour in retail outlets. He helps you understand just how smart some shops are. At the same time, you start to understand how so many could be so much better. I look at shop space now with a whole different view.

The Storytelling Animal: How Stories Make Us Human - Jonathan Gottschall

To communicate with customers, tell stories. To communicate with your team, tell stories. In fact, to get anything done in life, understand that the human brain is wired to tell and receive stories. It's how we communicate meaning. A must read.

Delivering growth

The Hard Thing About Hard Things: Building a Business When There Are No Easy Answers - Ben Horowitz

Ben Horowitz, Partner at VC firm Andreessen Horowitz, tells the story of his rollercoaster career as the CEO of a fast-growth tech company. He also shares some really important lessons learned. It's a riveting and insightful read, delivered with certainty from a VC who is usually right but will admit when he's wrong.

Good Strategy/Bad Strategy: The Difference and Why it Matters - Richard Rumelt

The subject line says it all. Rumelt is the world authority on strategy. I was lucky to meet him for lunch in 2011 and saw at first-hand how insightful a thinker he is. He maps out a framework for strategy and explains it using relevant examples from his decades of experience.

Anything You Want: 40 Lessons for a New Kind of Entrepreneur - Derek Sivers

This is a short, fun read. Essentially, it's a collection of blog posts from Derek Sivers, who founded (and later sold) CD Baby. There are some fantastic lessons to be learned here. I admire Derek for having strong convictions of what's right and wrong and how he applied this to business.

The Toyota Way: 14 Management Principles from the World's Greatest Manufacturer - Jeffrey Liker

Toyota introduced lean manufacturing to the world with the Toyota Production System (TPS). No matter what you think of Toyota cars, this is a fascinating insight into how the TPS came to be and how the company operates. The system is much, much more than a production methodology - it's Toyota's culture at work expressed in 14 management principles. Without these (often counterintuitive) principles, the system wouldn't work as well as it does - a real case of the sum being greater than the parts.

Kanban: Successful Evolutionary Change for your Technology Business - David J. Anderson

Kanban originally started out as a production management technique in Japanese manufacturing, but it is a great framework to use for software development teams. This book explains why, but more importantly explains how to get started.

Switch: How to Change Things When Change is Hard - Chip Heath and Dan Heath

How to effect change. Complex situations don't need complex solutions and you don't need to be a leader to make change happen. This book explores some principles of being a great change maker by telling stories of how change was delivered in some very interesting and challenging situations.

Reinventing Organizations: A Guide to Creating Organizations Inspired by the Next Stage of Human Consciousness - Frederic Laloux

This fascinating study of alternative ways of organising people to work together towards a common goal tells the story of companies that have renounced hierarchy and found other ways to collaborate and achieve success.

Personal Growth

The Chimp Paradox: The Mind Management Programme to Help You Achieve Success, Confidence and Happiness - Dr Steve Peters

Dr Steve Peters helped the British Cycling team to their Olympic gold medal haul by helping them focus on winning psychology. He helps you understand how your mind works and what you can do to deal with challenging situations. He uses this simple metaphor to explain: we all have a "Chimp" inside our heads as well as a "Human" and a "Computer". He shows us how we can recognise and handle our (sometimes troublesome) Chimp.

Thinking, Fast and Slow - Daniel Kahneman

Your mind and how it works. Kahneman explains how our brain responds to rational and non-rational triggers and how these complement each other. Human judgement is riddled with bias. This book is foundational reading for anyone interested in behavioural science. Developing awareness of your own biases (yes, you have lots of bias whether you like it or not) is essential to build self-awareness and therefore is a foundation for personal growth.

The Righteous Mind: Why Good People are Divided by Politics and Religion - Jonathan Haidt

This is a real eye opener. Absolutely fascinating. Just as we all have five types of taste (sweet, salty, sour, etc.), Haidt has identified through research five different flavours of morality which we all adhere to in different ways. We all have our own belief systems, and such is the nature of the way these flavours play out that there is no single objective truth, despite us all thinking we are right.

About the Author

David Norris is a seasoned internet leader, having worked in online operational, product, marketing and strategy roles since the turn of the century. This has been mainly in travel and hospitality, including four stints as Chief Operating Officer, three of which were scaling fast-growth venture capital-backed startups. He was later a VC investor at Forward Partners, incubating idea-stage startups, but now focuses on strategy and marketing in his role as Chief Growth Officer at Holiday Extras. David is also Non-Executive Director at The Sports Trust and mentors startup founders.

In his spare time, David enjoys travelling and being in the great outdoors. He's keen on sports beginning with S, being a keen skier, skateboarder and sailor.

He's in awe of adventurers and sporting heroes such as Amy Johnson, Ranulph Fiennes, Ernest Shackleton, Sky Brown and Ellen MacArthur, with their determination to take on adventure, challenge or adversity. He finds inspiration for new ideas by meeting new people and reading - he'll always have a book on the go and an idea brewing.

He lives with his family in Deal, Kent.

You can connect with me on:
🌐 https://norrisnode.com

Printed in Great Britain
by Amazon

30239290R10123